THE COMPACT HANDBOOK OF NEW TESTAMENT LIFE

THE COMPACT HANDBOOK OF NEW TESTAMENT LIFE

BETHANY HOUSE PUBLISHERS
MINNEAPOLIS, MINNESOTA 55438
A Division of Bethany Fellowship, Inc.

Originally titled *The World of the New Testament* and published in Great Britain by Ark Publishing, 130 City Road, London EC1V 2NJ.

Maps by Jenny Grayston

Copyright © 1979
E. M. Blaiklock
All Rights Reserved

Published by Bethany House Publishers
A Division of Bethany Fellowship, Inc.
6820 Auto Club Road, Minneapolis, Minnesota 55438

Printed in the United States of America

Library of Congress Cataloging-in-Publication Data

Blaiklock, E. M.
  [World of the New Testament]
  The compact handbook of New Testament life / E.M. Blaiklock.
      p.   cm.
  Reprint. Originally published: The world of the New Testament.
London : Ark Pub., 1979.
    Includes index.
    1. Bible. N.T.—History of contemporary events.
2. Sociology, Biblical. 3. Bible. N.T.—Criticism, interpretation, etc.
  I. Title.
BS2410.B56   1989
225.9'5—dc19   88–32754
  ISBN 1-55661-061-0   CIP

Professor E. M. BLAIKLOCK was Professor of Classics at the University of Auckland in New Zealand for twenty-one years. He was internationally known as a writer on classical and biblical subjects, and his numerous publications include books on Greek and Latin literature, the historical geography of the Mediterranean, biblical commentaries and translations, guides to the background of the Bible and archaeology. He also edited several major reference works before his recent death.

Contents

1. The Roman World 9
2. The Provinces 17
3. The Common People 31
4. Centers of Civilization 39
5. The Growth of the Empire 47
6. Travel in the First Century 55
7. Local Government in Judea 63
8. The Greek World 75
9. The Jewish World 95
10. The Pharisees 103
11. Sadducees and Essenes 111
12. Lessons for Today 119
Subject Index 129
Scripture Index 133

CHAPTER ONE

The Roman World

The Empire

The world to which Christ came was the Roman Empire. Geographically that formidable organisation, and the 'Roman Peace' which was its gift to man, took shape in the last score of years of the Emperor Augustus' life. When he died, at the age of seventy-six, appropriately on the nineteenth day of the month which bore his name, in AD 14, Jesus was nineteen years of age. The Empire, though it still lacked Britain, had frontiers as secure as it was ever to have, and the forty-four years of Augustus' virtual autocracy had given the world what it long desired – tranquillity and ordered government.

The Empire, as Rome and its ruler saw it, was, indeed, the world. Augustus had read of Alexander's march to the Ganges. He knew of far lands to the east whence traders returned, but it was no imperial arrogance to see a world of order within the rim of lands which surrounded the Inland Sea, safe beneath the shield of the legions. It is a small area on any modern map, and the Romans were not unaware of the fragility of the walls behind which their world lay. Inviting Maecenas, his patron and the Emperor's 'minister without portfolio', to dinner about 29 BC the poet Horace bids the statesman forget for an evening the problems of Spain, the Danube, the Euphrates. It is a stanza which casually reveals the deep preoccupations of those who bore the burden of authority. For many more years those questions fashioned their diplomacy, and determined policy. Augustus and his successor, all through Christ's

THE ROMAN EMPIRE IN AD 14

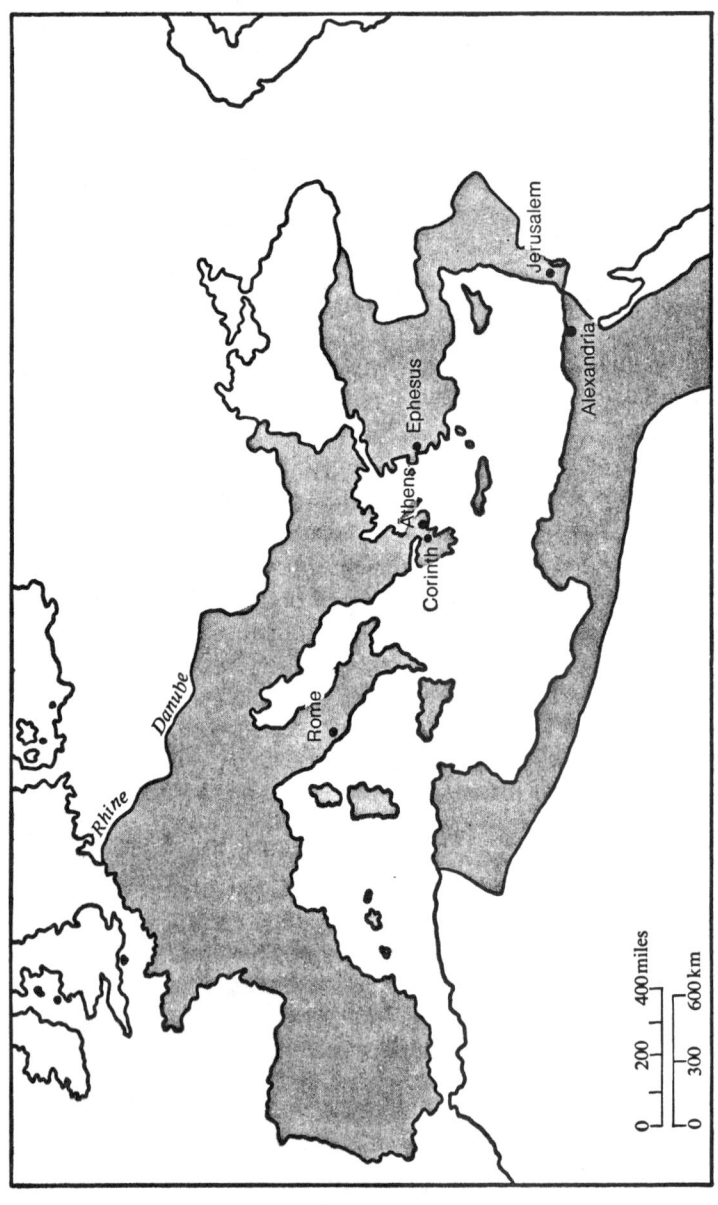

find the Sahara a firm frontier. There is no safer frontier than a desert, as Egypt has found through all the centuries. No one, including Rommel, has invaded Egypt from the western deserts.

It is easy to see how strong a roadblock, set between the sea and the sands, Judea and Samaria must have been in the mind of a security-conscious Augustus. Hence his wrath against Herod, who, in 9 BC, found occasion to fight a petty war with the Nabataeans. Their trading empire lay south-east, one remove behind Herod's domains, dominating the old 'incense routes' up which the queen of Sheba came, and the Wise Men of the Christmas story. In 26 BC, in one of her rare acts of flagrant aggression, dictated by no strategic need, Rome had been frustrated by the sands in a drive on Arabia Felix (Saudi Arabia and the Yemen today), an El Dorado, it was thought, of 'gold and frankincense and myrrh' (Matt. 2:11). Augustus wanted only quietness there, and, sensing some nervousness in that direction, Rome was soon to embark on a programme of fortifying the Red Sea coast of Egypt. Garrisons, archaeological investigation has revealed, dotted that arid coastal strip, which lies in heat and desolation between Egypt's ranges and the sea. It is difficult to see what peril they feared.

The one unclosed gap in the Empire's eastern defences, one not covered by impassable deserts, was on the northern horn of the Fertile Crescent, round and down the Euphrates plain. The warlike and half-barbaric state of Parthia lay beyond the twin rivers to the north-east, and the land of the New Testament was acutely aware of the danger it constituted. Many in Galilee could remember the horror of Parthian invasion, Herod included, for he had been a prisoner of the Parthians. During the last convulsions of the civil war which followed Julius Caesar's murder, and from which Augustus emerged as Rome's disguised dictator, those dreaded mounted bowmen had been raiding down the ancient trails. When Caesar fell, on the famous Ides of March in 44 BC, he was organising a definitive campaign against the Parthians. Rome, for her remaining history, never succeeded, by diplomacy or arms – and she tried both – to remove this menace to the eastern provinces. Rome's Mediterranean mandate clearly had geographical limits here, and it must not be supposed that the Empire, and especially the East, was unaware of the challenge. The scourge of a Parthian invasion haunts the imagery of Revelation (9:7-11), written, perhaps in the eighties of the century. The sting in the tail of those apocalyptic horsemen, the backward arrow which their formidable archers were trained to loose as they withdrew, was the famous 'Parthian shot'. The desert beyond the north-east approaches was not wide enough to check attack so swift and mobile. Fear lay that way.

The rivers

Beyond the ken of the eastern provincials, with their nearer concerns of security, were the north and north-western frontiers of the Empire, a live enough anxiety for those who sought to secure its peace. The frontiers to the north-west, thanks to the cruel and sanguinary Gallic campaigns of Julius Caesar half a century before Christ was born, stood firm on the Atlantic and the Channel. Britain, only touched in Julius Caesar's two not very successful reconnaissances of 55 and 54 BC, had almost another half century of freedom to run, until Claudius invaded the island in AD 43. The mountain tribes of Switzerland, an unpleasant, if not deeply menacing, salient into the northern defences, were still unsubdued, and northern Italy knew their occasional raiding. Gaul, by Christ's time, was well on its way to a remarkable Romanisation, paralleled by Spain and later by Britain itself. It was to help to shape Europe.

Augustus, all along the northern marches of Empire, had set to work methodically establishing Roman authority and security. Quirinius, as we shall presently see, was engaged on the pacification of the central Asia Minor hill-country, and feeling for the secure frontier the Black Sea only could provide, when he was called away to the task of supervising the delayed Judean census. The Emperor set the Rhine and the Danube as his boundary; unfortunately, the longest river-line in Europe. Drusus, one of Augustus' two stepsons, and the brother of the future ruler, Tiberius, was busy on an ambitious campaign to fix the frontier on the Elbe, a shorter and more manageable line, when he died on active service. It was 9 BC. Attempts continued with task forces battling through the difficult swamps and forests, until Varus lost three legions in a woodland ambush in AD 9. This discouraged Augustus, and he impressed upon his successors the need to be content with a fortified Rhine-Danube frontier. He thus made a crease across the map still visible today. Rivers are bad boundary lines, a fact which put the word 'rival' into the language for those who live on the same river, and therefore live in 'rivalry', amid the clashing interests which a common waterway provokes. The stockaded *limes*, as the Romans termed the northern limits of their fiefdom, were to prove the Empire's most perilous frontier, one doomed in the end to bulge and break, releasing the floods of outer barbary over the most remarkable system of imposed and regimented peace which man had so far contrived. That collapse was immeasurable catastrophe.

For all its rough handling of dissidence, the Roman system

brought peace to the vital decades which saw Christianity spread and take root. No one can imagine what history might have been had the Empire recognised the day of its visitation, had the villainous Nero never lived to initiate the sequence of events which led to the proscription and persecution of the Christians, and so left a Rome free to accept, in place of Caesar-worship, the unifying and transforming faith which came from the small province on its eastern marches. We can do no more than wistfully speculate what a predominatingly Christian Empire, socially compassionate, and outward-looking, with a peaceful culture eager to penetrate beneficently the forests, swamplands and nomad steppes, might have done for Europe. The Dark Age might have been averted, and modern Europe spared what Churchill called 'the rivalry of Teuton and of Gaul'. There might have been no German wars, and no tense dichotomy of East and West today.

The West

As it was, the decision which Augustus made to consolidate behind the rivers was taken and outworked largely within the brief lifespan of Jesus Christ. The lives of the apostles virtually saw its final rounding. Augustus was the true creator of what we call 'the West' today. When the Empire split in the fourth century, with momentous results for the church and mankind, the division was a distant ramification of Augustus' policy. Perhaps he wisely saw that Rome, as nations can, had reached the possible end of its outreach. Perhaps no other policy was possible.

Within those limits he acted well and effectively. He travelled widely when his hegemony in the capital was firmly placed to his satisfaction in loyal and trusted hands. He had a way of picking such servants. He sought, as he tells us in his own account (discovered cut on a temple wall at Ancyra), to make the provinces safe. The East, especially, accustomed to the worship of deified potentates, was quick to show its gratitude. Rome's own poets, Horace and Vergil especially, had been sincere and eloquent in praise. After a century of cruel insecurity and strife, man thought he had what man in his mass has always vainly sought, peace and safety. No age, more than our own, can better appreciate what such a benediction can mean. There are echoes in the New Testament. The Jewish hierarchy thought that they had discovered what Jeremiah had advised centuries before, that survival can sometimes consist in submission to an imperial overlord. 'Render to Caesar what belongs to him, and to God that which we owe to him', was a word they could not answer.

Augustus, when Christ was born, had gone far to consolidate what Rome had drawn into a whole. He had spread Romanitas behind firmer borders, and towns still living bear his name – Augsburg (Augusta Vendelicorum), Aosta (Augusta Praetoria), Autun (Augusto-dunum). Vienna (Vindobona), Buda (Aquincum), Saragossa (Caesar Augusta) were others of his memorials. His tidy mind now suggested that a worldwide census would be a useful assessment of his resources. He was not to know how difficult that would be in one small province, and how it would tangle with history beyond his imperial control, when he sent out his decree that 'the whole world should be enrolled' (Luke 2:1).

Chapter Two

The Provinces

The Land

Palestine was a word not commonly used by the Romans. It was formed from Philistia, and that name came from the Aegean, perhaps Cretan, people who settled in the coastal plain and built five cities, at the very time when the Hebrew nomads were infiltrating from the wilderness and the eastern hills. It was the first confrontation of Europe and Asia. Palestine was not clearly defined until the British mandate between the wars gave frontiers and clarity. The Romans thought rather of Judea and Samaria; principally of the former. They recognised minor kingdoms, and they held the province of Syria. It is significant that the terms 'Judea and Samaria' are appearing today in Israeli documents. When we think of Christ's native land, we do not go far wrong when we keep in mind the enlarged Israel of today and some of Jordan east of the river.

Like Bethlehem, 'small among the communities of Judah', the land to which Christ came was small, is still small, among the countries of the world. Size does not determine a people's contribution to history. Consider Athens' brief half-century, Renaissance Florence, and others too. None has given as much as Israel, from which the wonder of the Old Testament was wrought out of stern experience behind embattled frontiers. The wisdom of prophets and historians, shaped by the tides of strife, which swept those crossroads where continents and empires met, and their grasp of the inexorable moral laws by which societies rise and fall, found immortal expression in the literature of that one small land. The people of a land where the very stuff of education was history, history made, known, probed and felt in that same corridor of nations, could not fail to understand more deeply than others the terms on which man occupies his globe. Or so it seemed. It was, indeed, a land prepared for God's intrusion. Christ 'came home', said the author of the last book of the Bible to be written, 'he came to his own, and his own folk did not receive him' (John 1:11). Those who did receive him, however, the apostles of his choice, and those who accepted their message, broke into history for all time with the results of two millennia of dealings with Almighty God ...

Excluding the southern desert, Christ's homeland was the size of Wales, no bigger than the state of Vermont, Australia's Gippsland or New Zealand's northern peninsula – or, for that matter, of scarcely larger area than neighbouring Egypt's Qattara Depression. But it lay, as we have seen, across the converging highways of the Fertile Crescent, the horns of which touched the Euphrates and the Nile. Rome which, like Napoleon, saw Egypt as the key to the Mediterranean, never underestimated the importance of the small province, which was part of their unstable eastern frontier.

The instinct of the medieval cartographers, which placed Jerusalem at the centre of their world, was sound. What month has passed, this last half-century, which has not seen that part of the world high in the news? Christ came to the hub of history, though none could see it at the time. How seldom, indeed, is man aware of a day's significance! Where, in fact, is history made, and by whom? Augustus, anxious over the problem of succession to the principate, in grief over the family tragedies which had made that problem serious, could not have known, when Mary came on census-night to Bethlehem, that the issues of all history lay in a hill-town south of Jerusalem, and not in Rome where his modest home stood on the Palatine hill, and that it was his administrative act which made Bethlehem a town which all men know. And thirty years later could anyone have imagined that a Galilean teacher was choosing the makers of a long tract of human history along the north-western bays of a deep-set lake, where fishermen repaired their nets?

In Rome, the dour Tiberius, Augustus' last, unwilling choice, who had brought the bitterness of more than half a lifetime of rejection to the principate, was watching the river frontiers, jealous of his commanders still probing beyond the Rhine, concerned over unrest among the troops, eyeing Parthia, and fighting petty campaigns along the Saharan borderlands. He knew that the eastern frontier was difficult, and had thought to keep control of potential danger there by appointing to Judea a procurator; that is, a governor directly responsible to himself. He certainly did not at that time know that his designing commander of the Roman household garrison, one Seianus, had probably a sinister hand in that appointment, and that Pontius Pilate was to make a personal contribution to the long tragedy of Rome and the Jews. Rome, in the persons of those two brooding minds, the Emperor and his praetorian prefect, thought history lay in their hands, that they would shape the coming years. We can never know the issues of a day.

Bethlehem

And it was a significant day indeed when Joseph, the carpenter of Nazareth, read a notice in the village street which he knew from both family genealogies, his and Mary's, meant a journey to Bethlehem. It suited the Roman bureaucrats to gather to their place of family origin all who were to be recorded in the census. We possess such a notice sent out by the governor of Egypt, or at least the first paragraph. It is dated AD 104 and runs:

> Gaius Vibius, chief prefect of Egypt. Because of the approaching census it is necessary for all those residing for any cause away from their own districts to prepare to return at once to their own governments, in order that they may complete the family administration of the enrolment, and that the tilled lands may retain those belonging to them. Knowing that your city has need of provisions, I desire . . .

Jewish or Hebrew law coincided with the Roman edict. According to Num. 27:1-11 and 36:1-13, Joseph had to make his way to Bethlehem as well as Mary, for Matthew records Joseph's genealogy, and Joseph must have been considered Eli's son along with Mary, in the absence of brothers to Mary. This seems to be the reason for the two genealogies (Matthew's and Luke's). The two evangelists would hardly contradict each other. Mary had to marry within the tribe according to the regulations detailed in Numbers, and the two evangelists must have assumed that their variant purposes would be clear enough. There are other, but no better, explanations.

The imperial edict must have come to Joseph and Mary as a shocking surprise, for Mary had recently spent three months almost in sight of Bethlehem. She had sought sanctuary with her cousin Elizabeth at Ein Karem on a valley hillside, three miles west of Jerusalem. Bethlehem is six miles south-west. Had the ordeal of a journey half the length of the land not come with ruthless suddenness, would not Mary have remained within such easy reach of the place to which the Roman census called her? Surely, Nazareth called for a toilsome journey.

As it was, the pair arrived weary from travel, probably by the central main road through Jerusalem, where they would have briefly paused. Perhaps Hillel the great Pharisee, and Simeon his son, along with the famous grandson Gamaliel, had arrived ahead of Joseph and Mary. Pure conjecture, but there are tenuous arguments to suggest this relationship with David's line. Bethlehem, in any case, would have fathered many families, and would certainly have required special public arrangements, which the papyrus quoted was about to detail when it exasperatingly ends.

Mary must have thought of Rachel, whose tomb was near, where the little pastel-coloured town lay along the ridge looking down the long undulations of the sheeplands of Judea. It was near Bethlehem that Jacob buried his beloved wife. Mary and Joseph must have taken many days, with Mary, as the artists all insist, riding, as her son was to do, on a donkey's back. They passed through a long tract of history, for history lay then, as it lies today, on every slope and valley floor. Not only their Scriptures, but the very shape and fashion of their land reminded men of Israel of all their loaded past. It is impossible to escape the sense of age and deep significance there, and Joseph and Mary spoke of much as they rode down from Nazareth's edge of hills, across the coloured Esdraelon plain, up through the high country, past Omri's and Ahab's old fortress of Samaria (where collaborator Herod's temple to Augustus was rising simultaneously with his temple to Jehovah in Jerusalem), on through Jerusalem's tangled lanes, over the Mount of Olives, past Bethany, and south, to where Bethlehem lay curving on its brown ridge.

They must have been apprehensive, when they saw the crowds in the narrow streets. 'O little town of Bethlehem', runs the carol, 'how still we see thee lie'. Bethlehem was very far from being quiet that night. The host who had assembled in a town as old as Genesis must have seethed with resentment against Rome. All the beginnings of Palestine's disaster of eighty years later were there. The men of Bethlehem were Jews, who knew what that Roman census meant. In Bethlehem were the crowded faces of the story of the sermon on the Tabgha hillside, the Galilean seashore, the scene below Pilate's balcony, the foot of Calvary – and later along the invested walls as Titus' legions closed upon the city. They knew not the day of their visitation. They are infinitely pathetic, sheep with no shepherd, and searchers for that which was not bread. If indeed Hillel and Simeon were actually asleep in the inn, with the whole Old Testament stored in their heads, history was passing them by, as it was passing Augustus by in distant Rome, brilliant, able Augustus, his plans for peace and the vital transmission of power frustrated by a restless horse, by the sting of an anopheles mosquito, by the invisible invaders of the torrid east, which made fevers mount and wounds inflame. Augustus' heirs fell thus one by one, by accident, wounds, sickness. A hinge of history was turning, but not in imperial hands. But Augustus of Luke's cryptic verse was a great man. He had saved his country from the chaos of a hundred years. He had brought order out of the fearsome confusion which had followed the murder of Julius Caesar. He saw hope for the world only in a strong Rome, strongly led. He saw aright and for a generation he had ruled well. He did not know that his census had caused a prophecy of a Jew named Micah to be fulfilled, and that the crowded town in a restless province, not Rome by the Tiber, was at that moment the pivot of history. His chosen heirs were dead – Drusus flung from his horse, Gaius and Lucius dead of battle wounds and fever . . . and Christ was born.

The innkeeper of Bethlehem must not be misunderstood. He gave the family from Nazareth the best he had to offer. Picture a cavern in the rock. There are such hollows still to be seen there. At one end was perhaps a raised platform, where the host quite naturally, and with never a thought of slighting them, accommodated passing guests, in sight of their tethered beasts and stacked luggage. As a visitor of David's line, Mary might naturally have expected the best accommodation of the local hostelry. His *kataluma*, or 'guest room', which should not be translated 'inn', was already occupied. 'There was no room in the guest chamber.' The stable sleeping-place was his second best. The manger was a cosy rock-cut recess, or such stone troughs as may be seen today at Megiddo, or lying, half-finished, by the road near Magdala's deserted site.

Jeremiah (41:17) speaks of a certain *geruth*, or 'inn', which 'is by Bethlehem'. It was in the possession of one Chimham. Was this a descendant of Chimham, son of Barzillai, who, because of his father's beneficence to the exiled David (2 Sam. 19:31-38), was treated by the king as a son? Did he become thus, as the son of a great sheep rancher, the steward of the royal sheep-lands at Bethlehem? Did he build a hostelry, khan or shepherds' meeting place, which remained in the family after the unchanging fashion of the East, to provide a refuge in Jeremiah's day, and a rendezvous for shepherds still in New Testament times? The innkeeper could have been called Chimham or Barzillai, and conscious too that he was keeping up a tradition almost a thousand years old when he entertained those of David's line. We should not, then, imagine a harsh, preoccupied man who missed the great moment of his opportunity, but rather a harrassed host who did his best on a night of turmoil and distress to maintain an ancient family rite of hospitality. The cave under the Nativity church is probably the correct place, spoiled though it is by man's deplorable habit of cluttering holy places with the expensive trappings of devotion, and obliterating simple reality by massive buildings. Hadrian, doing his best to destroy the memory of all sacred sites in the land, and making no distinction between Jew and Christian, planted a grove to Apollo there, after the second great rebellion of the Jews in AD 132. He therefore unwittingly marked the site for the Empress Helena to discover, when the Empire surrendered officially to the faith, two centuries later.

To their accustomed place of gathering the shepherds came. Those who looked into the improvised cot at Bethlehem had strange premonitions, but no clear conception of what was to be. The shepherd visitors were a despised and lowly band. The rabbis' literature has many words of harsh contempt for their class. And yet it is part of the record of Israel that, when corruption and apostasy invaded high society, faith and truth found resting place and survival among the common folk of the land, the peasantry which sent Elijah and Amos to the court of wealth and decadence, the people of the ascetic communities, who produced John the Baptist to be leader of Palestine's greatest religious revival, such folk as those of Qumran, who hid their library, the Dead Sea Scrolls, in the wilderness caves. It is a pattern which history has seen recur, and in other lands than Palestine.

Nazareth

For the rest, it is more easy today to picture Nazareth, and the scenes of Christ's boyhood and youth, than it is to envisage Bethlehem. It is not at Mary's spring, as so often, hidden and sequestered by a superimposed church building, that we can imagine the realities of those almost hidden years of youth, but rather up the cluttered, crowded Arab *suq* in the old part of the city. It is narrow, as it may have been in the first century, with high pavements, and the traders' shops spilling into the street, and contributing to the drain-like interspace between, where burdened little donkeys plod.

Off to the right at the top of the slope is a tiny courtyard in front of a little cavern of a synagogue. Rebuilding may indeed have taken place, but the dim and echoing place looks ancient, and one surviving little pillar at the door seems at least a relic of some attempt at decoration, which a small village may have attempted. Small, Nazareth no doubt was. It finds no mention in the Old Testament, in Josephus, or the Talmud. Indeed, the very existence of the place has been questioned by some more sceptical scholars. It was overshadowed by Sepphoris to the north, and may have had no more than a hundred families to send their sons to the school in the synagogue. Here Jesus spoke one Sabbath day on Isaiah's words (61:1). The prophet had become the best known of all the ancient messengers of God in the land, thanks to John's preoccupation with his book. Perhaps, preaching as he did a few miles from the religious centre of Qumran, John had studied Isaiah from the very scroll which the Shrine of the Book in Jerusalem shows today.

The words bit deep. Nazareth's son had come home to the little town on the ridge, after a remarkable time in northern Galilee. They wondered, says Luke, at the gracious words they heard him speaking, but then the deeper and baser levels of human pettiness and jealousy broke to the surface. 'We know this man and his family,' they said. 'Therefore what worth beyond ours can he have?' They had seen him at the bench making the little wooden things they used, 'ploughs and yokes', says Justin Martyr, for an agricultural population. A 'carpenter' was a craftsman in wood, no plentiful commodity in those regions. The great timber trees of the Lebanon ranges were largely gone, for Solomon had taught his neighbours how to use their cedar for export earnings, and the greed of men used up the great cedar forests, as it has the redwood of California, and the kauri giants of New Zealand.

Isaiah speaks of a carpenter using one baulk of timber for a dozen purposes, some of it even for a crude household god, and it may be supposed that Jesus in his father's workshop, open to some little street, was economical in the timber he brought up from the port under Carmel or from some nearer local source. They had seen him at work, so how could he be in any way remarkable? And so they justified the question of Nathanael. 'Can any good thing come out of Nazareth?' – a town which had given Israel neither prophet, teacher, soldier nor leader of any sort? It seemed unlikely to the earnest man of Israel who, for deep sincerity, won the Lord's commendation (John 1:47).

And yet Nazareth had one gift to offer. Can we catch one glimpse of a boy's life in that little undistinguished town? In the wilderness of Judea above Jericho, he met the Tempter, who, from some place of eminence, showed him, and offered him, 'the kingdoms of the world'. There is no such prospect on the planet, so the vision must have been an adventure of the mind. A boy could go, on his way home from school, to some such vantage point on the rim of the hills as that where the E.M.M.S. hospital stands today. A vast half-circle of landscape would curve beneath. Hermon, splashed with snow, would be far to the left. The wall of the Carmel Range would be blue to the south-west, the end abruptly falling to the gap where Haifa stands today. Jesus could follow with his eyes the road which led across the Esdraelon Plain at his feet, forking either to the central hill-spine of the land and to Jerusalem by way of Samaria, or down the easier route, save for the final stiff climb to the Holy City, past the ruin-tell which must have been recognised even then as the fortress of Megiddo.

He could discern the Megiddo Pass, through which Thothmes III had led an Egyptian army against the Hittites on the Orontes, in the first recorded military campaign of history. The long lines of his marching men, their rolling chariotry and glancing spears, swung along and to the right to surmount the Ladder of Tyre. If there was one place in the Middle East where a brilliantly perceptive, fresh, young mind could grasp the whole pageant of history, it was near the place where the townsfolk thought to thrust him, years later, over the precipitous slope. After Egypt, Assyria and Babylon had marched that way, tramping over the old trails of Joshua and Gideon. And, if the air was clear, and not hazed by a sirocco out of Africa, the eye might just discern the thin line of green willows along the foot of Carmel, and even pick the half circle in the slopes far above, just beneath the line of the summit, where Elijah defeated the foul priests from Tyre and Sidon, and drove them down to the willow-lined Kishon for their execution. Alexander came marching south, three centuries before, Pompey north, when Rome came treading in, and Antony, mauled and defeated by the Parthians, staggered to Alexandria across that plain, when Joseph, who passed for Jesus' father, was a boy.

It is not for nothing that Armageddon, the gateway pass to that old parade-ground of empire, has assumed its apocalyptic power. And it was perceptive of General Allenby to choose Megiddo for his earldom, for with Megiddo in his hands he had won the last crusade.

Was not the temptation a vivid revival in Christ's mind of that scene of history, a vision of the nations, conceived in boyhood? And have we here, conceived admittedly in the imagination, a tiny flash of light on the hidden years, to set beside the real story of the boy left behind in the Temple, a story which Luke may have had from Mary herself? He had a long time while Paul was held in Caesarea to collect his information.

As the mind seeks to picture the little town on the hills where

Jesus spent his years of youth and early manhood, a healthy upland must be imagined, swept by the westwinds that poured in from the Mediterranean down the widening funnel of the Esdraelon plain. The Greeks called them the zephyrs, and they came waterladen to all the westward-facing coasts. Sometimes the precipitation was heavy, and the western areas of Galilee must have known such deluges as Elijah saw from Carmel, across the lowlands, when coiled thunderheads rose up like a hand with spread fingers.

Such a rainfall must have kept the waters pure, and taken away some of that preoccupation with water which haunted so much of the land to the south and east. Nor would Nazareth have the difficulties with water-supply which, in that world, dogged the big cities. One of Pilate's sensible acts of administration was to present Jerusalem with a good water-supply – a distinction shared with General Allenby, nineteen centuries later. Pilate's mistake was to finance his project from a sacred fund.

With a passing glance at the wider world of the day, it might be noted that there were other problems of public health connected with water pollution. Timothy, in Ephesus, was bidden 'take some wine for your stomach's sake, and your frequent bouts of illness' (1 Tim. 5:23). The advice would seem to indicate polluted water. Ephesus was an ageing and deteriorating city before Christ's time. Its harbour was silting from the man-made erosion of the hilly hinterland, and a sewer-system can be the first casualty of such damage. In Rome, where sewers of size and efficiency were known very early in the city's history, there were pollution problems of another kind. Lead was commonly used for reticulation, and lead poisoning, more especially among the upper classes, was common. Observe the creased and fallen-in cheeks of the Caesars – most noticeable in Julius, Augustus and Claudius. Loss of teeth, pallor and debility were noted by Rome's own Vetruvius as symptoms of such toxic conditions. Rome continued, none the less, to use lead, and even brought it to the provinces. Witness the lead piping at Bath in Somerset.

At Nazareth's synagogue, the teaching from the local rabbi must have been sound and based entirely on the Old Testament Scriptures. When the boy Jesus found his way to the conclave of the doctors of the law in Jerusalem, he astonished them both by his questions and his answers (Luke 2:47). Does his own teaching also reflect the teaching methods of the synagogue school? It was simple, and latched to features of life and of activity – the wind-flowers of the hillside, the tiny farms, fishing and commerce, all invading his parables.

Where, in the years of adolescence, was Joseph? He may have been, as tradition has it, older by many years than Mary, and have died, early in the hidden years. Life expectancy was low. A survey of the ages of death by natural causes, in the last half-century of republican Rome, where it is possible to abstract a few reliable statistics, shows sad brevity of life. The aged Anna in the Temple was a notable exception. It was not a healthy age. Observe the prominence of the sick and the ailing in the New Testament and the incidence of widows. In spite of the common sense which the great Hippocrates had infused into the practice of Greek medicine, and in spite of the calibre of men like Luke who were attracted into the profession, the standards of medical practice were low, and the general situation in the Lord's land in the first century must have been comparable with that of some of the less-favoured 'third world' countries today.

Famine, too, was becoming a chronic scourge. It was due to growing soil exhaustion in the eastern half of the Mediterranean and the fluctuations of drought in all lands which depend upon adjacent vast areas of desert for the patterns of their weather. Such violent movements may well have passed Nazareth by. She faced west, and was not harmed so much by the deforestation, caused by timber cutting and the depredations of the goat – a notable feature in Asia Minor.

Capernaum

The motives and the time when Mary, Joseph now presumably dead, moved with her family to the lakeside city of Capernaum are not known. The traditional site may be accepted with some confidence, and if Hadrian did destroy all the Galilee synagogues, he was not likely to have prised up the flagstones of the floor of the first building on the site. And in any successive building, the old stone would be sorted and stacked, as it is stacked round that precinct today, for recycling, and building into any new structure. Cut blocks and shaped lintels are not wasted.

In that case, what of the emblem of the two eagles, back to back, with necks flexed so that their beaks are together? A centurion, an officer no doubt of the famous Tenth Legion, appointed to that post for special qualities of understanding and character, gave the Capernaum Jews a synagogue. Did they find it impossible to object, in the face of such munificence, to the innocent desire of the generous officer to set the emblem of his legion in some place of prominence? He would hardly see their point about idolatry.

Capernaum was very different from Nazareth. The fishermen of the lake lived there, people of substance, and far from Prussian Frederick's 'dozen ragamuffins' of an irritated letter he wrote to Voltaire. The rabbis were plentiful and critical along the crowded lakeside. Capernaum was a customs post. Matthew was on the revenue staff. The lake separated, only narrowly, two worlds, Jew and Greek, and they mingled at all the road junctions. Here indeed was a place to meet man in his variety and need. Christ's first contacts were with the men who plied the most prosperous industry of the area, the fishermen who had been touched by John's revival far down the rift-valley. It is hard to exaggerate the breadth of the forerunner's awakening.

The date

But we moved ahead, and must pause to fix the boundaries in time of Christ's own world, beyond which we are not at leave to stray. Let us then in a page or two make some attempt to fix the date of census-time in Bethlehem. In the opening words of two chapters of his narrative which record in sequence the birth of Christ and the opening of his public ministry thirty years later, Luke speaks of events in secular history which give precision to his theme. Hence Augustus' census. Luke was not to know that the erosion of the years was to destroy all evidence but his own, that one Quirinius had held proconsular power in Syria more than a decade before the census of AD 6 or 7, to which Gamaliel referred as the occasion of much civil disorder in the land (Acts 5:37). If there was a census in those years it may be confidently stated on papyrological evidence that there was a census due 14 years earlier, conducted, it must be added, on the evidence only of Luke, by the governor Quirinius, a notable Roman aristocrat and soldier who died in AD 21.

Consideration of a problem which Luke quite unwittingly raised by his statement can begin with the sure assumption that Luke was a most competent historian. That reputation stands firmly upon the tested accuracy of his references to verifiable fact in his second book, the Acts of the Apostles. If, then, Luke appears to make Quirinius governor of Syria during the vital years of the nativity census, when it is quite definitely known that Quintilius Varus was governor of Syria from 7 to 4 BC, some other explanation than culpable inaccuracy on Luke's part must, in proper justice to no mean historian, be sought. If Luke said that there was a census in Judea at the time of Christ's birth, that statement, failing substantial evidence to the contrary, must be taken as fact, and the problems reduced to two. Why was the nativity census held so near the death of Herod in 4 BC? And how does it come about that Quirinius held, or seems to have held, his power in a large province of which the ill-starred Varus was the governor? Some small scrap of evidence, epigraphical or archaeological, might solve the whole problem. Ramsay thinks such evidence exists in an inscription found at Tivoli, which mentions a notable man who twice governed Syria in Augustus' lifetime. Quirinius would fit well, but it is certainty, not conjecture, which is required, and certainty is elusive in the absence of the actual name.

Observe that Luke merely says that 'a decree went forth from Augustus'. Between a decree and its execution, as Edmund Burke insisted before the English Parliament, in pleading for wisdom over the American colonies, 'months can elapse'. Indeed, in a world where communications were even slower than those of Burke's day two centuries ago, a very long time could elapse, given a resolute will to impede and to delay. Suppose Augustus, in 7 BC, issued his decree. It is already the spring of 6 BC when, by sea or land, the posts bring the order to Herod, who, a remarkable soldier and diplomat, but an evil man already touched by the paranoia which was to darken his ending, was in charge of Judea. He had lost Augustus' favour, as we know, in 9 BC, when, in defiance of his orders to keep a perilous frontier safe, he had fought the Nabataeans in a private altercation. Herod had, for amazingly long years, maintained his authority over the Jews, and his necessary subservience to Rome, in precarious equilibrium. The Jews, who had long since been reticulating the world with their synagogue communities, and travelling in hosts back home for the sacred festivals, would know that Herod had roused Augustus' ire, and that the Emperor had warned the puppet king that he would no longer be treated as a friend but as a subject. Josephus, in the closing chapters of his first book on the Jewish wars, gives a vivid picture of the difficulties Herod encountered as he strove to keep control. The very last thing which he wanted was the holding of a census. Perhaps Augustus, with something less than his usual wisdom, had made up his mind to bring Herod to heel. Right up to Hadrian, Roman rulers always found the Jews a problem, which baffled and exasperated them.

Suppose we attempt a reconstruction of events. Taking as long as he dares to make reply, Herod writes to Augustus begging exemption or postponement. The Emperor is adamant. Skilfully taking advantage of the delays caused by winter communications (compare Acts 27:9-12), Herod still temporises. A year or more could pass until Augustus, past all patience, takes over. The census must be held. Varus, in Syria, was the obvious man to take the task out of Herod's hands. He had a strong legionary force under his command, should the Jews prove fractious. One can imagine Augustus, a skilled, but not necessarily a hasty, picker of men, spending a few weeks considering Varus' capacity for a task involving the most wise and circumspect deployment of military force. Hesitation on Augustus' part was tragically vindicated in AD 9, when the same Varus lost his life and three whole legions in a German ambush. Flaws in Varus' military ability may have been visible in 6 or 5 BC. But, over the centuries, Rome had evolved a tried and effective system of superior and special commands. Some sixty years before, Pompey had cleared the Mediterranean of a pirate plague in three months, armed with special powers over the governors of all affected provinces round the sea.

Augustus, therefore, thinks of one Publius Sulpicius Quirinius, engaged at that very time pacifying some mountain tribesmen in central Asia Minor – not too remote from Syria and Judea. From Augustus' decision, to the time when Quirinius could receive his written mandate, wind up his operations in the highlands, journey to Syria, take over from a not very co-operative Varus a sufficient force of troops, and then hold the belated census, months would elapse.

October, 5 BC might seem a reasonable date. December 25 was, of course, Mithras' birthday, skilfully overlayed by the church. True, this reconstruction has no final proof backed by irrefutable evidence, but the solution does no despite to Luke's language. Its basic assumptions are fair, that there was a census at the time of Christ's birth, and that Luke was not likely to make a serious mistake about events which many living could remember.

For the rest, events in the narrative are true enough to existing evidence. We have quoted the Egyptian notice of AD 104. Actual census papers go back to AD 48. Here is the earliest example:

> To Dorion chief magistrate and to Didymus town clerk, from Thermoutharion, the daughter of Thoonis, with her guardian Apollonius the son of Sotades. The inhabitants of the house belonging to me in the South Lane are: Thermoutharion, a freedwoman of the aforesaid Sotades, about 65 years of age, of medium height, with honey-coloured complexion, having a long face and a scar on the right knee ...(*A missing line describes a second woman*) ... I, the aforesaid Thermoutharion (*the document continues with an affidavit*), with my guardian the said Apollonius, swear by Claudius Caesar Emperor, that I have assuredly, honestly and truthfully presented the preceding return of those living with me, neither a stranger, Alexandrian nor freedman, nor Roman, nor Egyptian, except the aforesaid. If I am swearing truly may it be well with me, if falsely the opposite.

Observe the identification by scars, which Thomas petulantly demanded. Scores of surviving documents mention them.

CHAPTER THREE

The Common People

The common people

It is the common folk of city and countryside who make history in any age. 'The Greeks suffer for the madness of their kings', wrote Roman Horace, thinking of the nameless men who rowed the 'thousand ships', and manned the walls and trenches, while Hector and Achilles fought it out at Troy. Rulers make decisions which affect a host of simple lives. They cross a Rubicon, invade an empire, demand a census, and swirling eddies sweep countless men and women down some torrent-bed of history. History seldom shows them to us. We can sense the exasperated crowd camping out at Bethlehem, can imagine angry faces jostling one man down a narrow street in Nazareth, can glimpse into a home or two in busy Capernaum or Emmaus. Surviving history from the first century, tragically little in bulk, in fact, is Rome-centred, save for the heavy but invaluable Josephus. It speaks of emperors, proconsuls, commanders, of frontier wars and the legions, who had found, in AD 69, what Tacitus called 'the secret of empire' – that an emperor could be set up in any army camp, a sinister discovery which was to bring final collapse.

But where, in the records, are the people whose ghostly presence can still be felt in the narrow streets of Pompeii and Herculaneum? Of surviving literature, oddly enough, only one large fragment of a novel survives to tell us anything of this nature. It is by an elegant figure called Petronius, an able governor of Bithynia, but principally the young Nero's director of pleasures, and known to the modern world from Henryk Sienkiewicz's brilliant portrait in his novel, *Quo Vadis*. It is a story which Petronius called *Satiricon*, a picaresque novel unlike anything else in Latin literature. The fragments which survive tell of the disreputable doings of three Greek scamps on the Campanian coast. If a comparison between works so disparate may be hazarded, Petronius' satire, Columella's *De Re Rustica*, and the Acts of the Apostles must be bracketed as the only surviving publications of Nero's principate which give some indication of a section of society outside the circles of Rome's dominant minority. Apart from being a storehouse for linguists of popular Latin, Petronius' novel shows the common life of that age of money-making and vulgarity, of low crime and shattered morality, among the poor and the undeservedly rich, in the market-place and the slum. One becomes aware of the Roman proletariat, of a populace going about its petty business and its varied carnality or the simple, innocent pursuits of each drab day, its joys and pain, the world of the Pompeian graffiti – and of the New Testament. There, if you will, is the world of the Gospels. It is as though the four evangelists had set out to do what John Masefield declared to be his aim in *Consecration*:

> *Not of the princes and prelates, with periwigged*
>   *charioteers,*
> *Riding triumphantly laurelled to lap the fat of the years,*
> *But rather the scorned, the rejected, the men hemmed in*
>   *with the spears.*
>   .   .   .   .   .
> *Others may sing of the wine, and the wealth, and the*
>   *mirth,*
> *The portly presence of potentates, goodly in girth.*
> *Mine be the dirt, and the dross, and the scum of the earth . . .*

He set out to write of 'the maimed, the halt and the blind in the rain and the cold', he tells us.

The Gospels

This, as documents of history, the four Gospels most certainly do. They reveal in enthralling detail what historians will hardly discover elsewhere – life in its raw simplicity. 'The common people', we read, 'heard him gladly,' and they move through the story, crowding the desert place, breadless as evening falls, listening on the seashore, casting aside fishers' nets to follow him and leave their names in history, blind, leprous, penniless, fathers with a competence, whose sons wander in some far country, housewives anxious over a lost coin, neighbours borrowing a loaf to feed an unexpected guest, labourers waiting anxiously in the market place to be hired for the day, women 'cumbered with much serving'.

Some have vanished almost without trace – the slaves, for example, on whose blood, toil, sweat and tears the economy of the ancient world was built. They found their way into the early church, for Paul himself, writing to Rome, sends greetings to those who were 'of the household of Narcissus.' Among the slaves of the base upstart who was the Emperor Claudius' freedman and confidential agent, there were, therefore, those who had found a faith in Christ, and gathered for worship with the first Christians of the capital. We know no more of them.

We touch another segment of commoner life in the Philippian letter, where Paul speaks of 'Caesar's household' (Phil. 4:22). This was probably the imperial civil service, which was growing apace, and of whose training school some epigraphical evidence exists. Some of it, in fact, suggests a Christian presence among them, and that evidence may include the cartoon scratched on a wall on the Palatine, where a small figure worships a crucified ass. The caption runs: 'Alexamenos worships his god.' The pupils were, no doubt, picked slave boys, like those Nebuchadnezzar set aside in Daniel's story, freedmen's sons perhaps, and any others promising enough to catch some official notice.

Again, the real people seldom emerge from the shadows of these lower strata of life. Onesimus is in somewhat closer view, a unique glimpse of a first-century slave. He robbed his master Philemon, in the Lycus Valley town of Colossae, somehow made his way to what Juvenal, the satirist of Hadrian's day, called 'the common sewer of the world', the city of Rome, was found destitute in some Tiberside slum, and sent home a Christian.

From the times which rise to view in the Gospels, events around 5 BC, and in the late twenties, it might be possible to assemble a few revealing papyrus documents from Egypt. The most famous would undoubtedly be the letter sent by a young husband to his wife in Alexandria, when Jesus might have been four years old.

> '... Hilarion to his sister Alis very many greetings, likewise to my lady Berous and Apollonarion. Know that we are still in Alexandria. Do not be anxious; if they really go home, I will remain in Alexandria. I beg and entreat you, take care of the little one, and as soon as we receive our pay I will send it up to you. If by chance you bear a child, if it is a boy, let it be, if it is a girl, cast it out. You have said to Aphrodisias 'Do not forget me'. How can I forget you? I beg you then not to be anxious.

The 29th year of Caesar, Pauni 23. (*Addressed*): Deliver to Alis from Hilarion.'

There is something peculiarly horrible about the casual directions for the exposure and murder of a babe in the context of an affectionate letter. Observe, from the new abortion statistics, how fast the world is returning to the grim days of pre-Christian times.

From several centuries of papyrus remains, it is possible to assemble some people of the street and countryside, such petty officials as 'the unjust judge', and 'the unjust steward', 'the prodigal son' and the rest. Literature generally, however, apart from the fragment of Petronius' novel, passes by this whole world of common life, those engaged on the petty tasks which make society function, who served in shops and dug the ground, built small houses, caught the fish and drew the water.

That is, all literature except the New Testament, which may be glanced at under two heads for the wealth of information its quite unique pages offer to the historian. Life as the proletariat lived it comes often into sharp focus in a hundred corners. Consider the host on the hillside above the great lake and the Tabgka Vale. They heard Christ talk within the circle of their narrow lives. 'Happy are the poor,' he said, and they all remembered Isaiah. The minds of all Israel were full of that prophet, for John's great preaching had been based on him, and the whole land had known the impact of the desert revival. The 'poor' form a common theme in Isaiah. Read the first eight verses of his twenty-fifth chapter, and the first verse of chapter 61, significantly Christ's text in Nazareth (Luke 4:18,19). In those days, in that land, poverty was more than physical deprivation and disadvantage. In popular religion the poor man was regarded too often as forsaken, for some good reason, by God. The poor man commonly believed this himself, and had a disastrous self-image. Daily, in perplexity and humiliation, he lived under what he thought was the wrath of heaven. Thus he was deprived of justice like the widow importuning the unjust judge. He was lowly, burdened in spirit (hence the phrase 'poor in spirit'). He hungered for recognition, for love. A ripple of hope ran through that listening multitude. And we catch one glimpse, wide as the lake below, of the sea of poverty.

They knew the burdens of life. Even rich men, legally faultless, failed too often to conceive the thought that great riches gave great opportunity to lift some load from all those overburdened shoulders (Luke 18:18-24). But here was one telling them to pray, even though their only privacy in some mudbrick house was the pantry (*tamieion*), the little lean-to built against the cooler side, where the poor supplies of food were kept (Matt. 6:6). It was good news to them when they heard that in such dark and humble privacy God would hear them.

They knew the agonies of life, what it was to return from the day's work in the field and find that some coward thief had broken through the fragile wall, and stolen some small possession which meant much (Matt. 6:19), or found that mice or moths had ruined some cherished and carefully stowed wedding garment. They knew the misery of flood sweeping into mud and sticks a small dwelling built in frailty on a dry valley floor, to be near some trail of petty trade. They looked up, as he spoke, and saw against the sky Safed on its hilltop, or to the east across the lake, Hippo on its conical mountain, cities both 'which could not be hid'. And the wild windflowers, delicately wonderful in a beauty beyond Solomon's robes, were all about their feet.

The whole scene is mirrored in Christ's words on the hill where today the little octagonal basilica stands among the magnolia trees. Here is another world, behind, beyond, beneath the 'princes and prelates', a world of work and toil, where a chance visitor required the borrowing of a loaf (Luke 11:5-8), and the whole street knew, when a tiny coin was lost in the straw on the hut's floor (Luke 15:8-10), and men stood about disconsolate waiting for a hard day's work (Matt. 20:1-16).

And as they sat above the lake, they could see the blue wall of the Golan Heights on the eastern shore. Beyond that lay the Decapolis, with its large Greek population where a boy from a farm could be lost, wasting the inheritance he was to have received in some brothel-lined and tavern-reeking street of Gerasa, whose marble ruins, theatre, forum, can be seen today twenty miles north of Amman – 'a far country' indeed.

There it is, in one sermon, the whole small world of Galilee, the farms with stony, eroded soil, and little tracks through the fields, where sparrows swooped to rob the sower, the dark cottages with a tiny shelf to hold a feeble lamp, the bushel measure in the corner to assess the crop anxiously before sale, the sin which haunts the meanest street at lower levels than its open commission, the stubble burned under a brick oven over which the sheets of dough were spread, the spinning wheel outside the gossipy door, the daily anxiety over mere sustenance, the salt dishonestly adulterated, or badly refined, and thrown into the narrow street, the blowing bits of chaff when the west wind down the Tabgka Vale swept the threshing floor. Where else in ancient literature can a canvas so crowded be found?

Read Luke, especially, who travelled Palestine well, and learn that Samaritans were free to come and go on business in hostile Judea (Luke 10:30-35). Or was the bitter hate of the northern brethren rather in the hearts of the hierarchy? But the roads were dangerous, with thieves on the boulder-strewn hillside. Jews went north, freely for the most part, through Samaria, and the Lord met a woman of their number by the Sychar well, a woman with the rudiments of information about the historic quarrel of their communities, and even some scraps of popular religion. And just as the Samaritan was free to trade down the winding Jericho road, so at Nablus the disciples could leave their master by the deep and ancient well, and go into the local market place to buy their midday meal.

We know from John that there were questing scholars, not too proud to seek an unknown teacher. There is Nicodemus to set over against Caiaphas. There is a glimpse, too, of the occupying forces. Rome kept them as far as possible out of the sight of the difficult and inflammable Jews, and the high command was shrewd enough to pick liaison officers with some sympathy towards Jewry, like the centurion of Capernaum, who actually financed a synagogue. Set him against the blundering Pilate, perhaps a deliberate *agent provocateur*, planted on that difficult frontier by Seianus, whose disloyalty was still unobserved by Tiberius.

Or catch a glimpse of rough humanity at the very foot of the cross. One of the execution squad in a gust of pity thrust his spear into the sponge which they had probably used to wipe the blood from their hands, dipped it into the jar of coarse ration wine which stood there, and lifted it to the lips of Christ. John (19:29) used a rare dialect word for 'spcar', a word which was easily corrupted by some early copyist. John, surely, wrote *hyssos*, and this became *hyssopos*. Hence our common reading. A crooked hyssop cannot provide a stick such as they saw, as Peter told Mark (15:36), from the back of the crowd. John, who was nearby, knew that the stick was a spear-haft, the head covered by the sponge. Note how meticulously both evangelists reported only what they saw.

But the point here is simply this. The legions march through the recorded history of the century from Caesar to Tacitus – 'boots—boots—boots—boots—movin' up and down again!' Only the New Testament in one short scene, shows us a gentler man amid the brutal soldiery, one whose senior officer looked up in wonder, and said: 'Truly this man was born of God.'

How familiar the whole scene is of the week leading up to Christ's death! The sense of the crowd, the vast faceless multitude which makes fuel and tinder for the demagogue, is as apparent in that first-century scene as it is in this present world, this 'mass-age' so vividly seen and anticipated by the French sociologist, De Toqueville, a century ago. A few words only detach themselves from the crowd round the place of execution. For the rest there was the vast inertia which is so visible today. The mass was composed of human beings, each drawn by his own motives, fears, hates, concerns, anxieties to the place where evil's triumph rose so high. But all alike were helpless, as the mass of men so often is. And worse, they formed a hiding-place, a stifling blanket, to cover and paralyse those who should have been seen in open testimony. In the anonymous crowd there were ten of the Lord's own men. Somewhere Judas was wandering. Perhaps Mark was there – a boy with a bandaged hand, if he indeed was the youth almost arrested in Gethsemane.

They had been more vocal when they followed Christ down the sloping, transverse path which led from the Mount of Olives, and again a week later. The chanting, shouting crowd in the street outside Pilate's place of judgement was another of the three crowds distinguishable in the story. In all crowds there is an 'activist' element, which determines action and gives the colour of its morality to the inert mass. At times the vicious minority stands apart, and acts as a spearhead. Such was the case on the road outside the Antonia Fort. Some of them there were the attendants of the priestly households, or the bribed clients of the Sadducees, perhaps resentful traders from the temple court, or others who found their personal advantage threatened. Others were those who, like Judas perhaps, found a passionate hope for insurrection, self-assertion, revenge, disappointed by a Messiah who had shown himself no royal figure, no leader of rebellion, but 'meek and lowly of heart', one who called to righteousness.

Wind and wave can be ruthless, and like wind and wave are those gales of emotion which sweep through crowds, and change a group of human beings into a destroying force. A crowd can be carried away by the consciousness of its own power, and the individuals which compose it are led to instincts which, apart and alone, each one might have held in check. It is intensely moving to read as simple history those closing scenes of Christ's ministry. Nowhere else does such revelation survive.

The New Testament narrative of the week of Christ's death became an historical record of first importance, both for this age, which is becoming fast the age of multitudes, and for historians who seek to understand the enormous tragedy of the Jewish rebellion. We can sense the climate. When the clash came in AD 66, and the awful years of the great rebellion began, it was all because of a crowd, swept by a storm of emotion, fanned to fury by its 'activist' element, which broke all control in Jerusalem.

We have seen base demagogues use crowds thus in our own century. The priests knew such trickery. They knew that reason dies in such heat, that which Germans call a 'group-personality' emerges, and that this can be a demon which will do the will of its creators. It is all the negation of justice, ordered thought, democracy. Tennyson saw the phenomenon emerging a century ago:

> *Tumble nature head o'er heel,*
> *and, yelling with the yelling street,*
> *Set the feet above the brain,*
> *and swear the brain is in the feet.*

The noisy crowd were as spurious when they shouted, 'Hosanna' as when they yelled: 'Crucify'. God speaks to individuals. How often, as the 'demonstration' moves down the street, do we catch the sound of the old evil! It is all in the Bible. How shockingly true is the New Testament, reserved, vibrating with reality. It was our world to which Christ came. 'We were there when they crucified the Lord.'

CHAPTER FOUR

Centers of Civilization

The cities

It should be with a sense of excitement and interest that any student of Roman history turns to the Acts of the Apostles. If he can do so unimpeded by the speculations of those who have expended too much sceptical ingenuity over the documents, and can come encouraged by some such assurance of the historical competence of the writer as that which, at the beginning of the century, converted W.M. Ramsay from sceptic to champion, he will realise with delight how illuminating a story lies in his hands.

A.N. Sherwin-White, one of the few modern classicists who have done precisely this, has written some enthusiastic pages on the theme. He notes the exactitude of the historical framework, the precision of detail of time and place, the feel and tone of provincial city-life, seen through the eyes of an alert Hellenist. 'Acts', he writes, 'takes us on a conducted tour of the Greek and Roman world, with detail and narrative so interwoven as to be inseparable.' Since Ramsay's well-known demonstration, Luke's fastidious regard for exactitude in nomenclature, and his sure handling of elusive fact are sufficiently accepted. 'I may fairly claim', wrote Ramsay eighty years ago, 'to have entered on this investigation without prejudice in favour of the conclusion which I shall now seek to justify... I began with a mind unfavourable to it... It did not then lie in my line of life to investigate the subject minutely; but then I found myself brought in contact with Acts as an authority for the topography, antiquities and society of Asia Minor. It was gradually borne in upon me that the narrative showed marvellous truth. In fact, beginning with a fixed idea that the work was essentially a second-century composition, and never relying on its evidence as trustworthy for first-century conditions, I gradually came to find it a useful ally in some obscure and difficult investigations.'

Ramsay first published this striking testimony in the Morgan Lectures of 1894, and then in the Mansfield College Lectures of 1895. A.N. Sherwin-White's confidence in the book was set forth in the Sarum Lectures of 1960, 1961. There are other classical historians who might also open wider eyes ... 'The narrative, in fact', writes Sherwin-White, 'shows remarkable familiarity with the provincial and juridical situation in the last years of Claudius. An author familiar with the later situation in Cilicia, and the final form of the judicial custom of *forum delicti*, would have avoided the question of Paul's *patria*, or place of origin ... The scene belongs unmistakably to an era which did not survive the age of the Antonines ... The evidence in Acts not only agrees in general with the civic situation in Asia Minor in the first and early second centuries AD, but falls into place in the earlier rather than the later phase of the development.' 'The author of Acts is very well-informed about the finer points of municipal institutions of Ephesus.'

Catch up the last words. To wander through the massively excavated ruins of Ephesus today is to sense the reality of the story. The great axial street, richly paved and colonnaded, runs from what was once the port, far though it is from the sea today, to the vast curving theatre cut into the hillside. The demonstration, another example of carefully manipulated mob psychology, began either in a market-place near the theatre, or in the silver-smiths' guild-hall down the main street. Codex Bezae, which retains some odd words and phrases not found elsewhere, pictures the scene as the inflamed mob poured 'into the street.' It is a vivid story.

The characters stand out: the two Macedonians, recognised as friends of Paul, and hustled down the street on the wave of the moving horde; Paul, cool as ever in a crisis; the provincial custodians of the Caesar-cult, the 'rulers of Asia' of KJV, not at all sorry to see damage done to the religion of Artemis; Alexander, probably a Hellenistic Jew anxious not to be exposed to unpopularity or pogrom because of the conduct of a splinter-sect. Observe too, the germs of coming conflict between the church and the proletariat, which Tacitus and Pliny, both provincial governors, note in their first secular accounts of Christianity. The metrical chant is almost audible, as it takes the place of reason in the collective mind of a mob, 'yelling with the yelling street.' Luke describes it with a phrase of classic irony (19:32).

Note, too, the sure touch of Luke's plural (38), which slips like a remembered phrase into his report of the city-official's political speech. 'There are proconsuls', the clever city clerk reminds the promotors of the riot. See this in the context of the speaker's anxiety over the privileged standing of his city with the ever-watchful imperial authorities, and another of the convincing marks of historicity emerges. The plural would seem to convey a touch of obsequious respect for the two imperial stewards, who, having murdered the proconsul of Asia, M. Junius Silanus, the great-grandson of Augustus, and therefore feared by Nero's base mother, must have been left with the administration of the province on their hands pending the appointment of a successor. There was only one proconsul in a province. Silanus' assassination was of Agrippina's devising, shortly after Nero's accession in the autumn of AD 54. Tacitus takes occasion to make a bald account of it in the preamble to his vivid narrative of Nero's principate. The tactful plural in the official's speech seems to be evidence in a single letter of the aftermath of political assassination, and the delicate relations between a 'free city' and Rome.

Ephesus, was, in fact, a sensitive point in the whole imperial

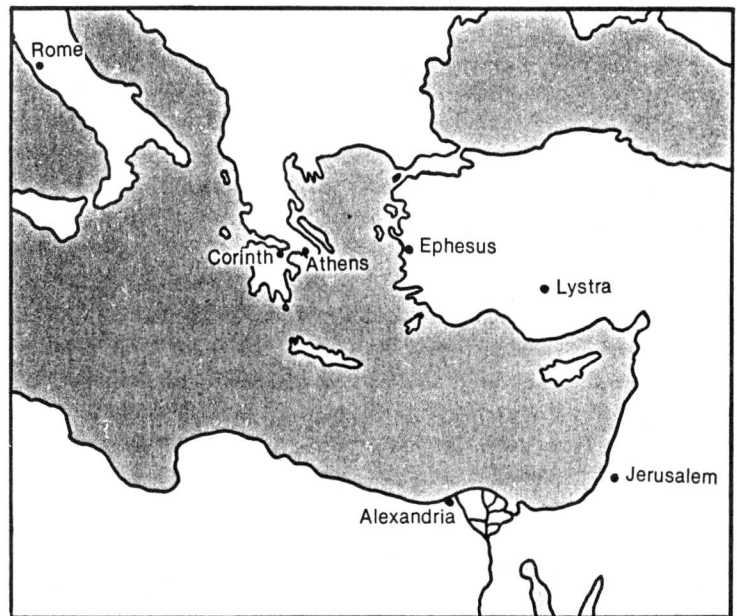

The main centres of civilisation

system, and it is interesting to see a responsible official concerned over the emergence of disorder there. There were other corners of the Empire where Rome could afford to overlook some measure of popular tumult, especially where local and responsible diagnosis could judge its incidence as harmless. Hence the significance of the story of Gallio, Seneca's genial and polished brother, and his cavalier treatment of the Jewish tumult in Corinth. In that cosmopolitan port the Jewish minority presented no peril, as it did in Alexandria, and a magistrate could afford an exhibition of Rome's liberal disregard of other laws than her own. Claudius' edict of expulsion of AD 49 was also a recent memory, and the ghetto, swollen by immigrant malcontents, may have been due for a rebuke. With such a breath of anti-semitism in the air, Gallio judged it wise to allow a brief outlet for emotion, as long as it was in full view and under control. Corinth was an important centre on a cross-roads of commerce, and it required a cool man, sure of support from the imperial government, to manage a riotous occasion with such quiet skill.

Sherwin-White, whom we have already quoted, has dealt with the point of legal procedure which the incident illustrates. Its more interesting significance is its demonstration of Rome in action. Her government was a rough-hewn art at this time, not a science based on text-book rules. The Romans were skilled administrators and imperialists. When a form of local administration was working, she allowed it to function, as long as peace was kept and the necessary dues were paid. Hence the toleration of the Herod family, scoundrels for the most part, but able. Hence the delicate balance in Ephesus. Hence the self-assurance of Gallio in Achaia in AD 52.

Nor did Rome expect to govern all her borderlands with rule-book regularity and with even-handed bureaucratic control. Lystra is an illustration of this. Popular superstition, based on a local legend of a theophany of Zeus and Hermes, led to an attack on two visitors, Paul and Barnabas, by a disappointed rout of native Lycaonians. There was no riot-squad to rescue the victims as Paul was rescued by Lysias, no city clerk voiced concern in a popular assembly, as at Ephesus. No proconsul like Gallio noted the outbreak of lawlessness with nicely calculated inaction. It was a remote edge of the Empire, a border-town with highland territory beyond, where pacification was marked rather by the absence of armed turbulence than by Romanised or Hellenised living. Cicero in Cilicia a full century before, Quirinius on the central plateau, just over half a century earlier, had dealt with back-country banditry by force of arms. 'Perils of robbers' formed a traveller's hazard in the blunt peninsula, and it seems clear that Rome did not expect to police its remoter borderlands as effectively as she policed Italy. Hence, perhaps, the bold murder of Stephen outside Jerusalem during some period of fortuitous or relaxed control by the occupying power. Rome in Judea deliberately kept the armed forces under control and, as already has been suggested, picked its officers with some care. All five New Testament centurions are men of worth. Pitiless during struggle, which often preceded her government, where, with nice calculation it was safe, she grew liberal in final control. How vividly Acts illustrates all this policy of government. The *politarchs* of Thessalonica, the *praetors* of Philippi, the 'first' of Malta all, by the way, demonstrations of Luke's careful reporting, are an indication of governmental adaptability and indigenous rule. The intelligent use of the Herods, the role of the Asiarchs, the functioning of the Areopagus, of which more presently, are severally illustrations of the same multilateral statecraft. Add the procurators and the 'free city' leaders in varied action. True, the glimpses we catch belong rather to the forties and fifties of the century than to the twenties, but the world did not change from decade to decade in those days. It is multiplying invention, and the surge and movement of great international developments, which cut those swathes through society which we call variously 'the generation gap', 'the new world', 'pre-war and post-war' – and which spawn what Toffler calls 'future shock'.

Rome was mightily altered in Augustus' day, according to the Emperor himself. He boasted that he had found it built of brick and left it built of marble, and indeed his huge building schemes, public and religious, were a part, and a not ineffective part, of his laudable attempt to revive ancient standards, the old ethos which he rightly judged had once made Rome great and strong. All the Emperors had some contribution to make. Nero sequestered a great area of the city after the Fire of Rome in July 64 to build his Golden House, and when Nero fell, the survivor of the dreadful year of strife, AD 69, used part of the site for the Colosseum, finished in AD 79. In such ways the capital changed.

It is none the less a fair guess that most of the ravaged city, like London sixteen centuries later after like disaster, was rebuilt on the old street lines, and that the Rome of Christ's day was very like the Rome of Paul's two imprisonments, and that both were not unlike the slum-ridden mixture of magnificence and crowded multi-storey tenements described by Juvenal in his Third Satire, at the century's end.

It is with some confidence then that we have looked at the cities of Acts and seen in the glimpses we have had of them a picture of the wider 'world to which Christ came'. We shall reserve Athens for consideration apart, for it will lead us to the Greeks, and the Hellenism which was a pervasive fact of the first century, and the very background of the New Testament, its language, its global religion, its great figures, Stephen, Philip, Paul. But one tract of Luke's narrative needs some further attention, for it shows a later chapter of an Israel visible in the Gospels. The choice of Barabbas was moving on to its inevitable conclusion, as we see in the later chapters of Acts.

Glance then at Judea again, where one of the great traumatic events of that century was taking shape. The Great Rebellion ranks with the civil war in Italy of AD 69, as one of the darker experiences of early imperial history. Tacitus has told the story of the grim struggle in some vivid chapters. Josephus' wordy Greek cannot obscure its utter horror. Vivid indeed are the scenes from a tense and heated province, where the coming clash, so precariously avoided in the mad Caligula's day, and made inevitable a few years later, is in full view. One can almost hear the orders in the briefing-room at Caesarea, before the alert tribune Lysias marched his cohort up to Jerusalem. Swift, sharp action by his trained riot-squad snatches their victim from the mob's lynching. And, a sinister revelation in a dozen words, the havoc cry which set the crowd roaring came from Asian Jews, who had seen an Ephesian with Paul in the Temple. Only a few weeks before, Paul had been forced to change his travel-plans because of a plot against him hatched by the Achaean Jews. The coherence of international Jewry, expressed and evident in more than one eastern Mediterranean city in the uprisings of both AD 66 and 132, is visible in both incidents. The passionate nation was a force to be reckoned with, world-wide. A man who openly declared a Roman citizenship was marked down as a renegade, and faced mortal peril all through the cities where Jews were settled. Restless tides of national consciousness were flowing. Claudius' expulsion of the whole Roman colony in AD 49 may have had some valid and weighty reasons in the mind of the ruler who wrote so sternly to the Alexandrian Jews in 42, in a surviving decree of exhortation and warning.

By the date of Paul's last visit to Jerusalem, the situation had deteriorated alarmingly. In the land itself, order in parts of the countryside must have practically collapsed, when it required an escort of four hundred and seventy men, as Luke reports, to slip one prisoner by night out of the turbulent city. The seventy cavalrymen in this task-force were no doubt the guard assembled to convey Paul down what was evidently a guerrilla-haunted road to Caesarea. It ran, as it still runs, under boulder-strewn slopes. Today the rust-proofed ruin of Israeli jeeps and trucks lie as a reminder of the changeless evils of human strife. The clash between the Jerusalem mob and the garrison which sparked the ghastly war was still six or seven years away, but the darkening stage was clearly set.

The Roman troops, who were doing all they could to avoid a confrontation, must therefore by this time have been practically confined to their strong-points and garrison-towns. Success in dealing with rural banditry, such as that which the florid orator Tertullus, no doubt with some justice, mentions in his preamble before Felix, can have been little more than a temporary alleviation of a gravely deteriorating situation. Festus' care to honour a puppet-king, whose selfless efforts to avert disaster were to be magnificently demonstrated a few years later, is also a pointer to the anxiety which was mounting in Caesarea. It was a clear error of frontier strategy to seek to hold so difficult an area with a garrison at Caesarea of only 3000 men, and the somewhat limited authority of procurators. The legate of Syria, who commanded the nearest legionary force, was too remote for the swift intervention which a crisis might at any time require. Rome's reliance on the able Herod family, already mentioned, is evident all through Luke's book, and was perhaps an element in that serious miscalculation. Perhaps the Empire overestimated the strength and hold of the collaborating elements. The policy of using available instruments of order meant that the Romans were prepared to overlook some abuse of authority. Stephen, as was mentioned above, was riotously stoned. Saul, with the Sanhedrin behind him, was permitted with impunity to arrest and persecute under arms as far as Damascus. All such activity was presumptuous under the rule of those who reserved and sequestered the power of capital punishment. It was being overlooked, provided, apparently, that illegal violence was channelled and directed against a proletarian minority on whose goodwill no vital issue of security depended. Rome could act, as her able officer Lysias demonstrated, with vigour and decisiveness when a critical situation suddenly demanded, and halt the action short of the provocation which precipitated disaster in AD 66 (Acts 21).

First-century history is therefore in deep debt to the New Testament, and historians must learn to read that remarkable corpus of documents with minds untrammelled by many of the difficulties which, of all people, New Testament scholars have themselves placed in their way. And of all the writers of the New Testament, Luke merits the greatest gratitude as a careful and meticulous collector and recorder of facts. The careful reader of the first five books of the New Testament has a very clear idea of the world of the first century in all its social strata.

CHAPTER FIVE

The Growth of the Empire

The Empire as a system

One pervading presence has filled the background of four chapters, and at this point there must be a closer look at the Roman Empire. At the outset we considered its geographical significance – a rim of provinces of varied depth surrounding, not without challenge, the Mediterranean Sea, but not the Black Sea, whose remoter coasts neither fleet nor legion could command. This was 'the world' which Augustus, its Emperor, was in the act of organising, securing, numbering when Christ was born.

It follows, of course, that the Empire was more than a fact of geography. It was a great geopolitical system, co-extensive with Mediterranean civilisation and its protecting hinterlands, a network of cultures and peoples conscious of vague and sometimes very present peril beyond the frontiers, and bound together by a common interest in security. It was peace which Rome gave and Christ came at the beginning of the *Pax Romana*, the 'Roman Peace', which took almost four centuries finally to crumble. Hence the unique regard, hardly to be paralleled in any other imperial context in history, which subject peoples held for Rome. Hence the urgency with which the cult of Rome and the Emperor was promoted in lands where 'divine' rulers were an ancient habit of thought.

With the hindsight with which historians inevitably look back, the Empire, as a system of order and rule, is dated from Augustus, perhaps from the Battle of Actium in 31 BC, from which Octavian, Julius Caesar's adoptive nephew, later dignified by the Senate with the honorific title 'Augustus', emerged the victor over a routed Antony. The danger of a divided Mediterranean world was postponed for three centuries or more. At last, after a century of disorder, military coups and civil strife, the world could breathe, ready to barter any elusive liberty for law, order, peace. A distracted world would do the same, perhaps, today.

That world, however, saw no sharp dividing line between the Empire and what it had to give, and the Republic which, in its expiring century of senatorial rule, had served the world so ill. Augustus, who simply called himself *princeps* or 'first citizen', had done no more than gather into his own hands all the old republican offices. He had even, in 27 BC, gone through the motions of 'restoring the republic'. The title 'Emperor' only represented that command of the armed forces which the President of the United States holds today. It was not for very many years that the title *imperator* became dominant. True, within Christ's lifetime, which continued through most of Tiberius' principate, the clever, concealed autocracy of Augustus was shedding some disguises. Paul knew Nero, John knew Domitian, and man's propensity for tyranny was then in full and odious view, but in Christ's world the mood was acceptance, save for the ever-intransigent Jews, a sense of relief rather than resentment. Paul, a Roman citizen, saw the Empire as a system to be won for Christ, and what if the Empire had chosen the enduring and preserving Christian cement? John saw the Empire turn tyrant, as Peter had feared (1 Pet. 4:7,12), and wrote the fierce poem of protest we call the Apocalypse. So dreams fade, 'and God fulfils himself in many ways'.

How it began

Legends surround the beginnings of Rome, some of them cleverly supplied by the Greek city-states which dotted the coastline of southern Italy. Aeneas of Troy was the founder of the Roman people, according to Vergil's great epic, and the city itself was the establishment of Romulus in 753 BC.

What is to be made of the old stories of Rome and her six kings? Simply that the Latin lowlanders of the enclave by the Tiber mouth, hemmed in by hill-tribes of similar racial origin, at some time in the eighth century united their strongholds on the volcanic spurs by the river-ford to found a federation ruled by one man. The marsh where they buried their dead, later to be the forum of Rome, may have prompted the thought that if the departed could lie in peace together, much more should the living unite for mutual protection.

Rome's six kings show the city emerging from legend into history.

A most ancient wall has left fragments still visible to attest the reality of the fifth of their number, and the Etruscan name of the last, Tarquinius, suggests that the small kingdom was dominated by the ancient kingdom of Etruria, which held central Italy. These were an Asian people, it seems, who had long held that area, and which, in Tarquin's day, had aged and weakened to the point that Rome could rise and throw off the alien yoke. The date was 510 BC.

A republic, aristocratically ruled by a Senate and elected officers, followed, a divided community in which the struggles of plebeians and patricians beat out the rudiments of Roman law. There was always a challenge on the frontiers, a challenge which only receded as Rome pushed those frontiers back against the northern Etruscans and the southern Samnites, and other opposing tribal groups. Perhaps that is why, for almost four centuries, the divided community which Rome certainly was settled its differences by law and compromise until a legal attitude towards life and politics became a fixed habit of Roman thinking.

A state now, of which the Greek communities took shrewd account, Rome thrust on in search of an elusive frontier of security, until all Italy was under firm control. Each new advance revealed new menace beyond, the Gauls of northern Italy, finally defeated in 283 BC, and a Greek invader from across the Adriatic a decade later. The Gauls a century before (387 BC) had, in one spasmodic episode, actually overrun Rome, and implanted that fear of the tribal hinterlands which was never to leave Roman consciousness.

In the middle of the third century before Christ, thanks to the island of Sicily, a bridgehead into Africa for Europe and for Africa into Europe, Rome had become aware of the great Phoenician commercial city of Carthage in North Africa. Greek communities held half of the triangular island, and Carthage the rest. A clash became inevitable, when Rome and Carthage persuaded themselves that the western Mediterranean basin was too small for two major powers. After twenty-three years of war Rome ended as a naval as well as a military power, and with Sicily and Sardinia as provinces. It was 241 BC.

Carthage set out to build a base and empire in Spain, and by 218 BC had found one of the great commanders of all time in Hannibal, who led his army into Italy across the Alps, and ravaged the peninsula for fifteen years. Rome at last realised that her armies could not defeat Hannibal in the field, and listened to Fabius Cunctator, the 'Delayer', who taught them how to hang on the Carthaginian's flanks, starve and weaken him, and cut off all reinforcements. Hannibal retired to Africa and defeat. It was 201 BC.

Rome now had Spain and southern France, still called Provençe, and had become aware of the danger from Greece, where Macedon was a power to be reckoned with. The eastern frontier was receding as the western had done. Behind Greece lay the successor-state of Alexander's divided empire, Syria, whose rulers had ambitions towards the west. After all, under Alexander, whose empire was divided in 323 BC, the Greek frontier had been the Adriatic, and since Philip II of Macedon, the father of the great Alexander, Greece had been a unit, not always subject to Macedon, but never able to unite against him, or to practise the city-democracy which Athens had invented.

During the grim days of the second war with Carthage, the Senate had ruled Rome well, but during the second century before Christ, with challenge on challenge drawing the Republic deeper and deeper into the east, it became evident that a rot had set in. Perhaps it was the vast bloodletting of that second war, perhaps the corruptions of wealth and power as Rome sought to rule subject provinces, perhaps it was the natural ageing and wearying of all mortal things, but certain it is that something great had died before the end of the second century before Christ.

Carthage had been eliminated in a cruel and unnecessary war in 146 BC, and in the same year Greece had been taught to obey by the equally vicious obliteration of Corinth. It was in 133 BC, the very year in which Attalus III of the Asian state of Pergamum bequeathed his kingdom to Rome in a vain hope to preserve it, that great constitutional challenges began to wrack Rome. Blood flowed in the forum in political strife for the first time.

Before the century ended a new fear was injected into the distracted Republic by mass invasions of Germanic tribes, a new fear, but really an old one, which half a century later was to lead to Caesar's eight campaigns in Gaul. Great commands were necessary to deal with great menaces. Great armies grew up owing allegiance to generals rather than to the state. Great temptations beset the custodians of great power. Great emergencies spawned extraordinary commands.

The dynasts

The last century of the Republic was a turmoil of civil war. It began with bitter strife between Rome and the Italian states, whose loyalty, unappreciated, had saved Rome in the grim days of Hannibal's invasion a century before, and who now sought what some enlightened Romans saw was just; parity, and common citizenship with Rome. The rebellion was brutally crushed but what the rebels sought was gradually conceded. The feature of the time was the emergence of dictatorial adventurers, some representing one side and some the other of those ancient factions in the Roman state, now rapidly polarising into something akin to Left and Right. Hence Marius and Sulla. Hence Pompey. A distracted Senate, faced with the threat of military coups at home and emergencies abroad, could no longer cope with the security problems of distant frontiers. Hence those extraordinary commands under which Pompey, in the middle of the century, cleared the Mediterranean of pirates and organised the east. Pompey was a true servant of the Senate, little though its greedy exploiters of a helpless world deserved his loyalty, and could, had he retained his army and the immense emergency powers he had been granted, have been the first autocratic ruler of Rome, an 'Emperor', anticipating Augustus.

Another star was rising, however. It was Julius Caesar, also armed, and driven to rebellion, as Pompey had been driven to disillusionment, by the folly of the Senate. First allies, then antagonists, Pompey and Caesar fought the first Civil War. Dictator at its end, Caesar despised the Senate, and swept it aside. He fell, on the famous Ides of March, 44 BC, under the daggers of senators who had no alternative policy to offer. Into the confusion which followed, stepped a nineteen year old boy whom everyone had forgotten, Octavian, Caesar's adoptive son, who arrived to claim his inheritance. Marcus Antonius, who sought, without the ability to carry the task, to be Caesar's successor, was outwitted by Octavian, who was uncannily able in his choosing of men. At Actium, in 31 BC, Octavian defeated Antony with the dangerous Cleopatra, Queen of Egypt, and the forces of the east behind him, and averted a division of the Roman world, which might have done immense harm.

Octavian, later to be honoured with the title of Augustus, was more shrewd than his adoptive uncle. He covered his autocracy with the forms of the Republic. He avoided all notion of kingship, which for five centuries had been anathema in Roman ears. Rather, he secured power by concentrating in his own hands the great republican offices, and by so dividing the government of the provinces that the Senate could comfortably live under the delusion that it shared the rule of the Roman world, while he himself could retain control of the frontier provinces wherever an army was required.

It was a fragile arrangement, as Augustus knew. He sought in vain (baffled, as we have seen, by disappointment and tragedy) to provide a successor. But the provinces welcomed peace after turmoil, and the prince could set about building the frontier walls and seeking in a not ignoble way to revive the old Roman spirit of stern morality on which, he rightly diagnosed, all Rome's greatness had been built.

Ennius, first of Roman poets, had once said:

> The commonwealth of Rome is founded firm
> On ancient customs and on men ...

Great Greek observers, like Polybius, had agreed. Roman history was for thoughtful Romans a deep preoccupation. Their own history was for them the only history worth narrating, or as Collingwood put it, 'not one out of a number of possible particular histories but universal history, the history of the only genuine historical reality, ecumenical history, because Rome had now, like Alexander's Empire, become the world.'

And thoughtful Romans, in Christ's time, knew that something vital had died. Cicero, who was murdered by Mark Antony in December, 43 BC, in the grim aftermath of death which followed Pompey's and Caesar's war, quotes those lines of Ennius and comments:

> Our poet seems to have obtained these words, so brief and true, from an oracle. For neither men alone, unless a state is supplied with customs too, nor customs alone, unless there have also been men to defend them, could ever have been sufficient to found or to preserve so long a commonwealth whose dominion extends so far and wide ... But though the republic, when it came to us, was like a beautiful painting, whose colours, however, were already fading with age, our own time not only has neglected to freshen it by renewing the original colours, but has not even taken the trouble to preserve its configuration and, so to speak, its general outlines. For what is now left of the 'ancient customs' on which he said 'the commonwealth of Rome' was 'founded firm'? They have been, as we see, so completely buried in oblivion that they are not only no longer practised, but are already unknown. And what shall I say of the men? For the loss of our customs is due to our lack of men, and for this great evil we must not only give an account, but must even defend ourselves in every way possible, as if we were accused of capital crime. For it is through our own faults, not by any accident, that we retain only the form of the commonwealth, but have long since lost its substance ...

Cicero, whom Byron called 'Rome's least mortal mind', did not live to see the subtle Augustus infuse the forms of the republic into an autocracy, but his words were prophetic. He would probably not have approved of Augustus' political stratagem, but he would have been the first to admit the need for what Augustus sought, by his programme of promotion for the old gods of Rome, to effect. The great patriot historian of Rome, Livy, whose writing occupied the whole of Augustus' principate, had some interesting words to say in his preface, which could have been written, of course, at any time during that period. A great task lies ahead, writes Livy, but 'it will be a satisfaction to have done myself as much as in me lies to commemorate the deeds of the foremost people in the world' ... He continues:

> Here are the questions to which I would have every reader give his close attention – what life and morals were like; through what men and by what policies, in peace and in war, empire was established and enlarged; then let him note how, with the gradual relaxation of discipline, morals first gave way, as it were, then sank lower and lower, and finally began the downward plunge which has brought us to the present time, when we can endure neither our vices nor their cure.
>
> What chiefly makes the study of history wholesome and profitable is this, that you behold the lessons of every kind of experience set forth as on a conspicuous monument; from these you may choose for yourself and for your own state what to imitate, from these mark for avoidance what is shameful in the conception and shameful in the result. For the rest, either love of the task I have set myself deceives me, or no state was ever greater, none more righteous or richer in good examples, none ever was where avarice and luxury came into the social order so late, or where humble means and thrift were so highly esteemed and so long held in honour.

A feature, then, of the world to which Christ came is visible. It was a world weary of its past and ripe for a new religion. The two great poets, Vergil and Horace, are evidence of this. A new religion was to be offered to a world without a frontier from the Atlantic to the deserts beyond Damascus, from the Rhine and the Danube to the Sahara, a world interpenetrated by Jews, Greeks and Romans, a world with a common second language, reticulated by roads, where travel had never been more easy. It is the great tragedy of history that Christianity as Paul conceived it and expressed it was rejected. Certain it is that in no earlier century could the Christian gospel have moved with such ease throughout the world. At no earlier point in Mediterranean history could the amalgam of Judea, Greece and Rome have as effectively cohered to form the New Testament, Paul of Tarsus, Christianity itself. And, let it be added, it is clear to all who with perceptive eye read what Romans were saying from the middle of the last century before Christ to the middle of the first century after his birth, that never before was man so conditioned by disillusionment with the past, and the breakdown of old moralities, to reach for hope and a better future, a more fulfilling faith.

This fact is too little taken into account by the historians who write the story of the Empire. It was early in this century that Sir William Ramsay, archaeologist and classicist, sought to underline this truth. 'They devote', he said, 'an occasional footnote, or a paragraph, or even a special chapter, to what are called "Persecutions". The one overwhelming factor in the situation of the Empire was its relation to the church. In their reconciliation lay the only hope of permanent growth. A large portion of the most hardworking, eager and resolute people in the most progressive provinces, were estranged from the government and exposed to intermittent and incalculable risk . . . This portion was, on the whole, the educated middle class, the real strength of the State. The government, by estranging this class, was throwing itself unreservedly on the support of the soldiers.'

A century of history had shown that such a course led to increasing convulsions, weakness and death. In the New Testament we see Paul's hope of winning the Empire die. The sixties saw it pass, and the alienation which produced the fierce protest-poetry of the Book of Revelation take over. The crop of the Empire's folly did not begin to ripen, much less be reaped, until past the time which we are looking at in this brief study. But it is visible in its beginnings and needs mention in a chapter which discusses how the Empire came to be, and to contain within itself, as most things human do, the seeds of its own decay.

CHAPTER SIX

Travel in the First Century

Communications

Before passing to the other great political and ethnic reality of the time of Christ – the Greeks of the Greek Dispersion and Hellenism – a brief consideration should first be given to a fact already apparent, the unity of the Roman world. Augustus' decree was issued by that able and cautious ruler in no mood of megalomania. It indicates that, in his mind, there was a stability, and a nexus of authority, wide and comprehensive enough for him to begin a statistical survey of that which was contained within the frontiers, on which he had worked for a full score of years.

It is fascinating, as was remarked at the end of the last chapter, to look back, survey the centuries, and observe the convergence of historical processes at the beginning and on into the first century. A certain historical precision accompanies the loosing of the Christian gospel on a unified world. The spread of Roman authority eastward was as complete as it was to be. The door to the Asian steppes was blocked by the Parthians, as interested as Rome was herself to stem any surge westwards of the barbarians of the hinterlands. It was a weakness in the Roman system of security that neither diplomacy, nor arms was able to do what Julius Caesar's genius might conceivably have done, and incorporate that powerful and half-barbaric empire into the Roman world. But having lost a vast opportunity to sweep west when Crassus' three legions were wiped out at Charrhae (Abraham's Haran) in 53 BC, Parthia was quiet enough, apart from one deep raid into the Middle East, to give no great trouble during the vital generations which saw the beginnings of the Christian Church, and its diffusion through the Empire.

It is even possible that Judaism and Hellenism, the two contributors to the New Testament, were influencing the Parthian tribesmen. A performance of Euripides' *Bacchae* was on the boards at the Parthian court in 53 BC, for the actor, who was playing the relevant part, used Crassus' head for that of Pentheus in the grim play. And among the Jews of the Dispersion, who heard Peter at Pentecost, were Jews from Parthia (Acts 2:5-11). They were no doubt from urban ghettos, but those conglomerations of the scattered race extended into Egypt, where Jews formed more than half of the population of Alexandria, and even further – to the Malabar coast of India, for example, where communities of Jews may have existed since the days when Solomon's trading partnership with the Phoenicians sent Tarshish ships on the west monsoon, and back on the eastern, to fetch the luxury cargoes of 'gold and ivory and apes and peacocks' (1 Kings 10:1-22).

Add the Yemen, whence sizeable immigrant numbers of Jews have joined modern Israel. Ophir was probably there, the land of 'gold, frankincense and myrrh', and the Magi, who came to Bethlehem, were perhaps the cultural posterity of Jews of Solomon's Golden Age, who followed the old incense route down to Shabwa and Arabia Felix, whence the royal visitor came to visit Solomon, to wonder at the wealth of his court, and spawn a corpus of legend.

Apart from these uncongenial and difficult avenues of escape to the eastern ghettos, there was no means of withdrawal from the authority of Rome, to claim or seek any form of political asylum beyond the frontier. For good or ill, there was no escape. Onesimus from Colossae was picked up in the capital, and happy though the outcome may have been for that one escapee, it may have been disaster or death for many unrecorded unfortunates. The dissident or the fugitive was, in Gibbon's words, 'encompassed with a vast extent of sea and land, which he could never hope to traverse without being discovered, seized and restored to his irritated master.' It has already been pointed out that Paul was recognised in the Temple by Ephesian Jews, and that Apollos, Aquila and Priscilla demonstrate great mobility, from Pontus on the Black Sea to Rome itself. And James chides the age-old rushing to and fro of businessmen (Jas. 4:13). Lydia was selling purple cloth 600 miles from home in Thyatira (Acts 16:14).

A Macedonian (perhaps Luke himself) formed the substance of Paul's dream at Troas (Acts 16:9-12), and to respond to the invitation meant no more than looking for a ship in the dockyards, crossing the Aegean, and walking up the Via Egnatia to Philippi, where Paul, a Tarsian with Roman citizenship, had considerable political privilege.

People were, then, mobile and travelled in all parts of the Empire for trade, Lydia for dyed woollen cloth, Aquila and Priscilla for the goats' hair cloth known as *cilicum*, from the province of Cilicia, Paul's own. They came to Jerusalem for worship, such as Simon from Cyrene (Mark 15:21); to Athens to lecture or to hear lecturers, a practice documented from the days of Plato to Paul (Acts 17:21); to Ephesus and Corinth to frequent the temples of Artemis and Aphrodite ('Not everyone,' ran a Greek and Roman proverb, 'is lucky enough to go to Corinth'); to Epidaurus and to Pergamum for the healing 'incubations' of Asklepios; to Olympia, Corinth and Delphi for the games; to Capernaum for the hot springs (perhaps that is why Christ found so many sick there). There were plain tourists, if Pausanias' guide books of the next century are an indication. Paul was, no doubt, not the only provincial who went to Jerusalem to study under a famous teacher.

Roads

Christ and his small band followed tracks and byways rather than roads, if conclusions may be drawn from the names of the villages they encountered on the way. On his one excursion out of truly Israelitish territory, the visit to Tyre, a pathway over the hills from Galilee must have been followed, with no frontier impeding. The Roman road system was still under development in the areas of New Testament missionary travel, and it is known that the army engineers had built thousands of miles of roads in the regions roughly designated Syria and Palestine by the early years of the first century.

The Christians, indeed, were appreciative of the fact that travel was easy in the Empire. 'The Romans have given the world peace,' said Irenaeus, 'and we travel without fear along roads and cross the seas wherever we wish.' The Golden Milestone, set up in Rome, was, by the end of the first century, the point from which roads radiated to the Antonine Wall north of the Scottish Lowlands, to the Euphrates and Jerusalem. Milestones measured their every reach. Strong as the legions, they ran straight and firm through mountains and over rivers, raised above flooding by their tirelessly engineered foundations and flagstones. Says Gibbon in his stately prose: 'They united the subjects of the most distant provinces by an easy and familiar intercourse, but their primary object was to facilitate the marches of the legions ...' But the travelling Christian used them, too, whether it be Paul, or Philip on the desert road through Gaza, which must have been surfaced at least sufficiently for the progress of a chariot. Paul trod a Roman road through the Cilician Gates, across the peninsula of Assos, up to Philippi, and the Via Appia, oldest road of all, up to Rome (Acts 15:41;16:12;20:13,14;28:15). If Paul endured 'danger from robbers' (2 Cor. 11:26), and if the Jericho road was unsafe, this was in corners of time and place where order had not yet been made firm or had broken down. The dangers against which Lysias took large precautions, when he sent Paul under heavy escort to Caesarea, were due to a fanatical plot, and to the fact that, under some lamentable procuratorial misrule, the area was moving fast towards the fearful disaster of the Great Rebellion.

Ships

Travel by sea, if not trouble-free (2 Cor. 11:25,26; Acts 27), was common, and the engineering of considerable ports was almost equal to anything which could be produced today. Herod the First spent twelve years, from 25 to 13 BC, building the port of Caesarea, for example, as a base and bridgehead for the Romans who kept him in power. It would tax today's highly mechanised society to build a mole of limestone rocks, some fifty feet long, forming a breakwater in twenty fathoms of water 200 feet wide. The dry docks for the galleys are still visible. And Caesarea was tiny compared with Alexandria and its Pharos lighthouse.

For the great ships which traded in the Mediterranean, we can turn to the wall paintings of Pompeii and Herculaneum, the cities which were destroyed in the great eruption of Vesuvius in August AD 79. They must depict vessels roughly contemporaneous with the Alexandrian grain-ship which brought Paul and his fellow detainees to Rome, under the escort of a military courier cohort, known as the Augustan regiment (Acts 27:1). It appears that these vessels differed little in the general shape and pattern of the hull from the common ship-designs of the next eighteen centuries, except that both ends were similarly shaped. The contour was straight along the middle, sweeping high at both ends, and often terminating in structures like the backward-bent neck and head of a goose. Hence the term *cheniskos*, for the stern of a ship (from Greek *chen*, a 'goose'). In one of the Pompeian tombs, the device expands into the head of Minerva, to form something like the figurehead of more recent times. Paul's ship from Malta to Rome may have been similarly decorated with Castor and Pollux, the Twin Brethren who protected sailormen. Isis decorated the prow of a ship described by Lucian in the middle of the second century. Three friends are speaking in Lucian's dialogue, Lycinus, Samippus, and Timolaus. They decide to visit the Piraeus, the port of Athens, where a big Alexandrian grain-ship had taken refuge from a bout of stormy Aegean weather. The visitors stood a long time by the mast, counting the hides in the sails. They marvelled at the dexterity of a sailor who went up the rigging, and ran out along a yardarm holding the ropes. The vessel was 120 cubits (180–220 ft) long, a quarter as wide, and from deck down to bilge twenty-nine cubits (43–53 ft.). Anchors, capstans, windlass, cabins all amazed the Athenians. They estimated, perhaps a little extravagantly, that her cargo of corn could supply Attica for a year. 'And all this', Lucian makes one of his characters say, 'a little old man had kept from harm by turning the huge rudders with a tiny tiller.' The tonnage is estimated by those who understand such calculations as 1938 tons.

Timolaus had a talk with the captain who had survived the *meltemi* in the Aegean, and brought his ship safely into the port. The passage, like one or two other accounts of storm at sea in ancient literature, serves to underline the reality and authenticity of Luke's superb account.

Josephus asserts that he once set out for Rome on a ship which carried 600. 'Our ship foundered', he writes, 'in the sea of Adria and our company of 600 souls had to swim all night,' He was one of eighty picked up by a ship of Cyrene, who 'outstripped the others and were taken on board.' The last words are very like Josephus, who had a fine instinct for personal survival, at the expense sometimes of others, and before doubting his figures it is well to remember that archaeology, especially at Masada and round Jerusalem, is going far to establish the reliability of Josephus.

Winter sailing was commonly avoided, and mid-September to mid-November was considered a particularly perilous period. It was probably the autumnal heat of the Sahara sucking southwards the masses of chilled air which were building up, at that season, in central Europe. Paul's shipmaster used this airflow to make a swift trip down to Crete, and then hoped, sheltered by the 140 mile barrier of that island, to make Fair Havens. He was defeated by the eddies and down-draughts caused by the highlands of western Crete blocking and distorting the continuing northerly gale. From then on, it was a battle to keep a westerly course, and avoid the Syrtes, the shoals in the oblong bay on the African coast, which underwater archaeology shows to be a veritable graveyard of ships. The undergirding of the ship was secured by cables, probably carried for the purpose, which enmeshed the hull and could be tautened to save

MAIN TRADE ROUTES IN THE FIRST CENTURY

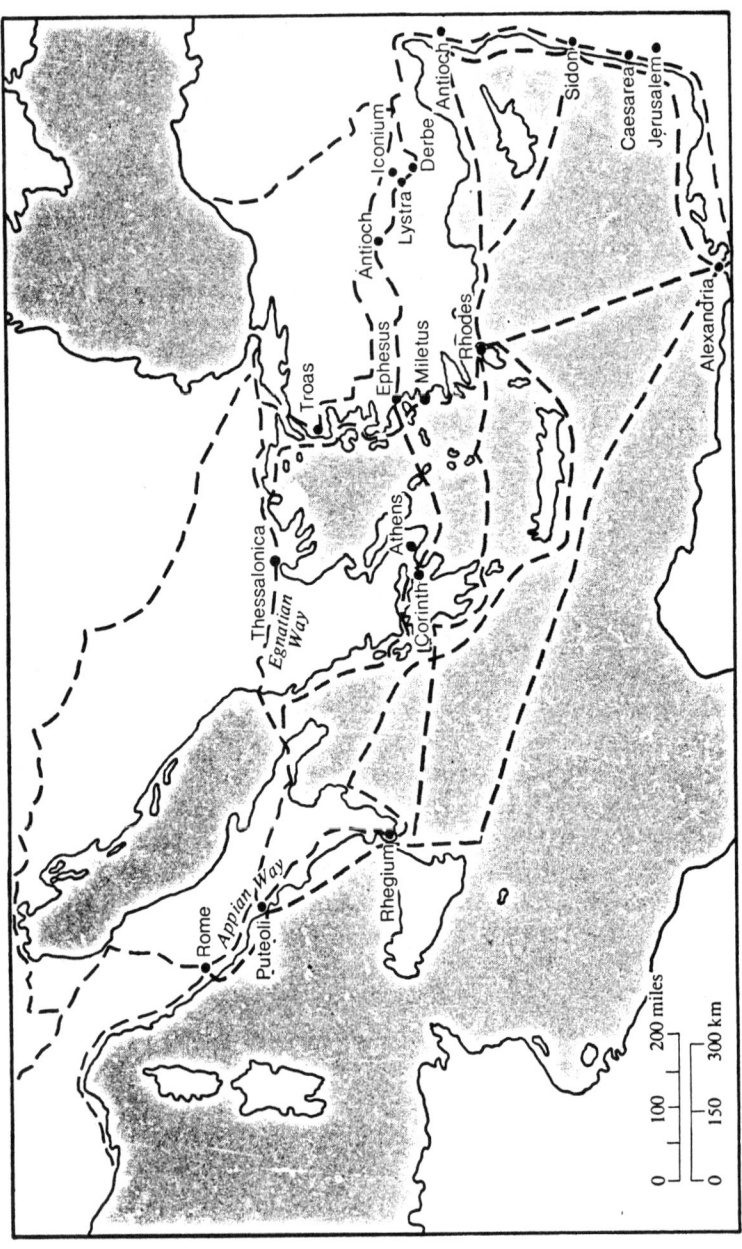

the timbers from opening as the mast strained against the keel and its lateral supports (Acts 27:17).

It would appear that rival shipbuilding among the Hellenistic kings of the second and third century before Christ had kept alive a tradition of Mediterranean shipbuilding which went back to the 'ships of Tarshish', probably the heavy, strong-hulled galleys the Phoenicians built for the Spanish iron-ore trade, and named after Tartessus in Spain. If the legend of the boy Jesus' visit to Britain with Joseph of Arimathea is true, it was in a 'Tarshish ship' that he would have sailed. For the rest, he knew only the boats of the Galilee lake, probably low, sturdy vessels like the caiques to be seen today on the Aegean islands, designed to carry a load of fish, and survive the blusterous squalls, which the air conditions in the Jordan Rift valley bring about. The accounts in the Gospels do not suggest boats of great size. One could sleep, apparently, in the stern. They could hold a dozen men, and an unusually heavy load of fish could be a problem to them (Mark 4:38; Luke 5:7).

Sailing times are difficult to calculate. Luke has too few clues to make it possible to calculate, but it might be a fair estimate that a good day's sailing might be fifty miles, and that one would need to reckon a three months' voyage from Tyre or Alexandria to Rome. This, as was suggested when discussing the census, would have given Herod a considerable scope for delaying tactics, even if imperial posts used sections of the road network and the facilities provided. To proceed down Italy by road to Brundisium, to cross to Dyrrachium and cover Greece by the Via Egnatia, was not to say that shipping would be immediately available at the vital ports at the end of the journey.

All in all, in matters of population movement, emigration and travel, the world of the first century was not unlike our own. Speed, of course, by which we can 'put a girdle round the earth' in twenty-four hours, has mightily accelerated; comfort, a modern demand, is always available ... Apart from that add travel and the dominance of cities to the features which make the first century more like the twentieth than any of the others which fall between. The comprehensive variety of Paul's missionary strategy was a phenomenon of the first century. Neither a century before, nor a century later, for different reasons, could his diligent implantation of the Christian church within the accessible framework of the great Roman system have taken place.

Chapter Seven

Local Government in Judea

Roman imperial administration in the provinces was glimpsed as we have looked at some of the Greek cities of the first century and discussed the New Testament as a revealing document of their daily life. It is inevitable in any discussion of the geographical and historical background of the New Testament that the theme should move back and forth between the narrow world of the Gospels and the ministry of the Lord, and the wider world where Jew and Gentile moved. This wider world was the arena of the evangelistic endeavours of Paul, along with the unrecorded world evangelism of the other apostles, planting churches through the whole network of the imperial system.

As well as the pervasive political presence of Rome, we must eventually look to the subtler influence of the Greek Dispersion. First, it is necessary to devote some space solely to the subject of Roman government and administration in Judea, for both the trial of Christ and the trial of Paul were mingled with it, and the closing chapters of the first five books of the New Testament are revealing light on the conduct of three procurators in office, and confrontation with unusual difficulties, difficulties, in such a context, inevitably political.

Procuratorial rule was instituted in Judea, on the deposition of Archelaus in AD 6, with Coponius as the first procurator. He was a well-to-do Roman, and something, it may be supposed, of a career diplomat. He it was who held the controversial census of AD 6 with the aid of the legate of Syria, Quirinius. It provoked widespread dissidence (Acts 5:37). It has been argued above, in discussing the date of the Nativity, that Quirinius must have had earlier experience of this dangerous operation, and Gamaliel, addressing the Sanhedrin a generation later, had vivid memories of its political repercussions.

Procurators were not powerful men. They were direct appointments of the Emperor to provincial areas of some danger, but in which a large military presence was considered, for some reason, not a dire necessity. In this role they governed Thrace and Judea, but in a wider circle of provinces they were senior aides under the direct control of a proconsul. In the case of Judea, the rule of a procurator was a bad miscalculation on the part of Rome. Rome however was not the only nation, from ancient times to modern, to find the Jewish nation clever, passionate, desperately patriotic, difficult to manage. That turbulent little province really demanded the rule of a special administrator with military power at his immediate disposal, and trained wisely to use military power. The special status under Augustus of the governor of Egypt shows that Rome was not unable to devise and operate such a scheme.

The Jews were bemused by history. They held a 'promised land'. Nor had they forgotten how, in the era between the Testaments, they had risen and flung off the alien rule of Syria, one of the four 'successor states' of Alexander's wideflung empire. The Books of the Maccabees tingle with the heroism and spirit of that struggle. The Lord himself had warned his people against their misguided and earthly messianic hopes (Matt. 24:23-26), so tragically illustrated in the brave and infinitely sad story of Masada, still a symbol in Israel. 'The Spirit of Masada', as every discerning visitor learns, is still a potent factor in modern Middle Eastern politics. *Shenith Masada lô tipol* is a soldier's oath still sworn – 'Masada shall not fall again.'

To commit a people so conditioned to separatism and nationalism to the comparatively weak rule of procurators, small men, armed with no more than half a legion almost confined to barracks at Caesarea, was a risk which the Empire took. Had it succeeded it might have been used to demonstrate the political wisdom of the Empire. It failed, and one reason is that the procurators, court favourites, diplomats by profession, senior civil servants, were ill-equipped for a task so subtly difficult, and were perhaps under orders to hide, where possible, the mailed fist.

This is what makes the New Testament so revealing a document of imperial policy and government as three procurators move briefly on to its prominent stage. We should have known little of any of

PALESTINE IN THE FIRST CENTURY

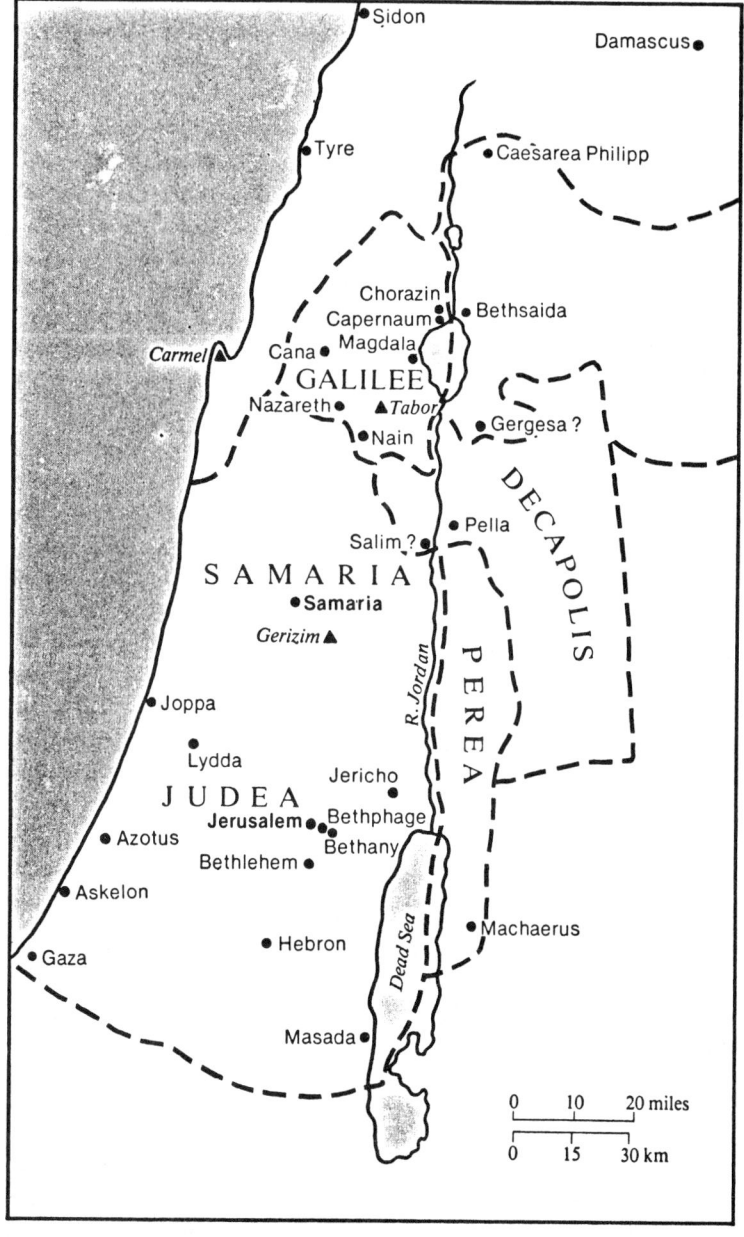

them had it not been for their involvement with the beginnings of the Christian faith.

Pontius Pilate

First, then, let us turn to the case of the governor who surrendered to 'the Jews' (a term to be discussed later) and crucified Christ. To study Pontius Pilate is to encounter on a small stage an omen of history. Here was Rome choosing a policy for other reasons than justice. Here was Jewry calling for that blood upon its head and on its children which most surely came. Here was Jewry choosing Barabbas in an ecstasy of folly which led straight to Titus' siege. And here, too, is a picture of a Roman governor under Tiberius at odds with his province, and fighting desperately to be rid of a problem which threatened his career, and perhaps his life.

Tiberius, Augustus' dour successor, was not easily handled, and Pilate faced that day's situation gravely compromised. It is difficult to know whether the Roman blundered into the feud with the Jews, which so tied his hands, or whether, in arrogance and contempt, he had deliberately provoked the passionate race with offensive acts, underestimating the subtle minds of his priestly opponents. Pilate's coinage suggests the latter interpretation. The procurators had the right to issue small coinage in the province of Palestine, but it was considered sensible, in designing coins likely to be in the hands of multitudes, to avoid deliberate offence. Coins were always far more significant to their ancient users than they are today. They were a means of instruction and propaganda, and were studied carefully for what they had to say. The authorities generally had a strong appreciation of the fact.

The story of Christ and the tribute-money shows that the Emperor's portrait, with the offence involved, was in use, but the silver denarius was issued as tribute-money, and accepted as such. This was Christ's point – accept Caesar's peace and you must accept Caesar. It was a different matter to put out a mass of copper coinage which ran counter to Jewish sentiment, but that is what Pilate did. Valerius Gratus, Pilate's predecessor, had struck coins harmlessly adorned with palm-branches, or ears of corn, familiar enough Jewish symbols. Pilate issued coins as early as AD 29 bearing the *lituus*, or pagan priest's staff, a symbol of the imperial cult bound to be obnoxious. It is difficult in this to see anything short of deliberate provocation but it was safe insolence, because the coin-users were provoked individually, and the coinage was not likely to produce collective demonstrations of hostility. The story of the tribute-money does show that the Jews had a bad conscience about the

Roman currency. They had accepted the imperial coinage, and were carrying its implied idolatry around. The provocative coinage was withdrawn after AD 31, and that year saw the fall of Seianus, Tiberius' disaffected prefect of the praetorian guard, the plotter whom the old Emperor tumbled from his post of dangerous eminence by an act of consummate cunning. One is left wondering whether there is something in the suggestion, already mentioned, that Pilate was a protégé of Seianus, and that some of his arrogant folly was his patron's suggestion.

The Pilate, however, of the provocative coinage is undoubtedly the Pilate of Josephus and a less reliable Philo, and certainly the Pilate of the Gospel narratives. Josephus may be left to tell the story of the standards:

> 'Pilate being sent by Tiberius as procurator to Judea, introduced into Jerusalem by night and under cover the effigies of Caesar which are called standards. This proceeding, when day broke, aroused immense excitement among the Jews; those on the spot were in consternation, considering their laws to have been trampled under foot, as those laws permit no image to be erected in the city; while the indignation of the townspeople stirred the country-folk, who flocked together in crowds. Hastening after Pilate to Caesarea, the Jews implored him to remove the standards from Jerusalem and to uphold the laws of their ancestors. When Pilate refused, they fell prostrate around his house and for five whole days and nights remained motionless in that position.
>
> 'On the ensuing day Pilate took his seat on his tribunal in the great stadium and, summoning the multitude, with the apparent intention of answering them, gave the arranged signal to his armed soldiers to surround the Jews. Finding themselves in a ring of troops, three deep, the Jews were struck dumb at this unexpected sight. Pilate, after threatening to cut them down if they refused to admit Caesar's images, signalled to the soldiers to draw their swords. Thereupon the Jews, as by concerted action, flung themselves in a body on the ground, extended their necks, and exclaimed that they were ready to die rather than to transgress the Law. Overcome with astonishment at such religious zeal, Pilate gave orders for the immediate removal of the standards from Jerusalem.'

Note in this incident a blend of arrogance and cowardice. The ensigns surmounted by an eagle and bearing Caesar's image offended a Jewish prejudice based on the second commandment. Why was Pilate so provocative? Perhaps he clumsily sought to honour the dangerous old Emperor. Perhaps he indulged a superstition of his own, which weighed more in his mind than a superstition of the

Jews. At any rate, the incident was a lesson to the Jews. They had summed up their governor, and knew that his arrogance could be overridden by clamour, and that his cowardice at a certain point asserted itself.

Some time later, if we are to believe Philo, the Alexandrian, in a matter passed over by Josephus, Pilate tried again, timidly or obstinately, to honour the Emperor where he had not been honoured before, in Jerusalem. In Herod's palace he hung some gilded votive shields dedicated to Tiberius. The reaction was violent. Pilate faced immediately a deputation of the Sanhedrin, and the four surviving sons of Herod the Great. The latter group, exploiting the influence their family had always enjoyed in Rome, appealed to Caesar, when Pilate proved obdurate, and Tiberius sent a curt order to his governor to move the shields to Caesarea, and hang them in the temple of Augustus. It is easy to see why Pilate was shy of a further complaint. He had handed another advantage to his foes.

A third incident shows the same mingling of cruelty and timidity, the same inability to cope with the Jews. Josephus tells the story:

> On a later occasion he provoked a fresh uproar by expending upon the construction of an aqueduct the sacred treasure known as *Corbonas*: the water was brought from a distance of 400 furlongs. Indignant at this proceeding, the populace formed a ring around the tribunal of Pilate, then on a visit to Jerusalem, and besieged him with angry clamour. He, foreseeing the tumult, had interspersed among the crowd a troop of his soldiers, armed but disguised in civilian dress, with orders not to use their swords, but to beat any rioters with cudgels. He now from his tribunal gave the agreed signal. Large numbers of Jews perished, some from the blows which they received, others trodden to death by their companions in the ensuing flight. Cowed by the fate of the victims, the multitude was reduced to silence.

Such is the background of the trial of Christ. The story in the Gospels is rapid and tense. It seems clear that Pilate had agreed with the priests that the early morning trial and condemnation was to be a mere formality. His wife, disturbed by her husband's vicious compromise, dreamed a dream, and her hasty note stirred the superstitious feelings of Pilate (Matt. 27:19). In an effort to gain time he attempted to open the trial formally, and enraged the priests who had no formal reply ready, and had expected no such formalities. Compromised by his past mistakes, in the grip of his latent cowardice, forced to act without delay, a prey to his Roman conscience, which knew that an innocent man was being betrayed to death, Pilate fought to free Christ on a legal subterfuge, sought to thrust decision on another, one far too astute for such a piece of trickery (Luke 23:6,7), endeavoured by the dramatic symbolism of hand-washing to clear his soul, and finally surrendered, as he did before, to passionate clamour, and revealed the familiar arrogance by his superscription on the cross.

And so for a few brief hours, to be followed almost minute by minute, history's spotlight played on a minor Roman governor. He was a forerunner of more exalted rulers in the Roman imperial system who were to betray justice, persecute the good, fail to see the nearness of deliverance, and lose the road to safety. The scratched marks on the Pavement, under the Convent of the Sisters of Zion, is a microcosm. Pilate diced for his soul and lost.

It was Rome's participation in the hierarchy's crime that ensured that Christ died on the cross, and not by stoning, the Jews' way of inflicting judicial death. The bones of poor Yehohanan Ha-Gaqol, dug up in their ossuary at Givat Ha-Mitvar in 1968, show how a crucified man died. A great nail, its point bent in a knot of olive-wood was through both twisted ankles. The two bones of the forearms were scratched as the young victim, crucified a few years before Christ, struggled to lift himself to exhale and snatch a mouthful of air ...

But we can leave the story there. We are looking at the world of Christ's day. Here was the darker side of the Roman Peace. Here was one of the Empire's servants in a world too large for him, manipulated by collaborating elements who were essential to his task of holding a frontier and counting cheap a human life. It is a glimpse to be paralleled nowhere else in literature, of imperial Rome at her worst – as the story of the polished Gallio in Corinth shows her at her best.

Antonius Felix

Almost as remarkable is Luke's story in Acts of Antonius Felix and Porcius Festus ... It was fortunate for Paul that the canny Roman authorities had built the four-square keep of the Antonia Fort in such a way that it could play unobtrusive sentinel to the Temple courtyard at the corner of which it stood. Paul was also fortunate in the type of man who was in command of the garrison. Claudius Lysias seems to have been one of the career men frequently met in the days of Claudius' notorious two freedmen ministers, Pallas and Narcissus. Claudius, a social misfit in the imperial family, had acquired some unorthodox friends in his association with those who accepted him, a palace substratum of money-making and vice. Lysias was a Greek, as his name indicates, and his first name was acquired when, at the price of a considerable bribe, a piece of corruption common enough in that venal group, he was granted the still coveted Roman citizenship. On the other hand Lysias seems to have been a vigorous and capable soldier, with good relations with his staff (Acts 22:26). The centurion is at ease with his commander.

Felix, into whose custody and protection Paul now fell, was, like Pilate, a lamentable mistake. All sorts of irregularities disgraced his governorship. He was the brother of Pallas, the notorious freedman and senior minister of Claudius, already mentioned, an upstart of whom Tacitus, the biting Roman historian, speaks with blistering scorn. He is no less contemptuous of Felix who, he said, 'thought he could commit every sort of iniquity and escape the consequences'. He felt secure under his powerful brother's shadow. Nothing could be more untrue than the opening gambit of Tertullus' artificial oratory (Acts 24:2,3). We have seen what state the country was in from the fact that Lysias detached the major part of a cohort to secure the safe arrival of Paul in Caesarea. The countryside must have been in a state of anarchy.

Such was the man before whom Paul preached of 'righteousness, self-control, and judgement' and who put off consideration of such things until a 'more convenient season'. Tacitus mentions him again in describing the events which led up to the rebellion. He describes him as 'a master of cruelty and lust who exercised the powers of a king in the spirit of a slave.' Nero recalled him in AD 56 or 57, and he passes from the scene of history.

The scene in court is dramatic, a striking illustration of the lines of James Russell Lowell:

> *Truth forever on the scaffold, Wrong forever on the throne,*
> *Yet that scaffold sways the future and behind the dim unknown,*
> *Standeth God within the shadow, keeping watch above his own.*

For a brief moment Felix seemed to have been touched with fear, and faced himself. He is visibly confronted with a crisis and makes a decision. His greed for bribes was the last factor which turned the scales. There is no 'more convenient season' than the passing moment when the vital choices of life are to be made.

Felix was tangled in a web of his own weaving. As with Pilate, it would have taken a mighty act of the will to rise and cut himself free. He was unable to make that painful reappraisement and died as he lived. But historians must be grateful for this small glance inside the walls of the immensely strong port and garrison town of Caesarea Maritima, Caesarea-by-the-sea, to distinguish it from Caesarea Philippi, at the Banyas source of the Jordan.

Citizenship

The conversation between Paul and the garrison commander is another of those revealing passages which make the Acts of the Apostles so notable a document of Roman history. It will be appropriate at this time to glance at what Roman citizenship meant. It depended primarily on birth but from earliest times could be conferred by legislative or, under the Empire, administrative, action. Indeed, generally speaking, Rome was extraordinarily liberal in sharing and extending the privilege. By AD 212 all who lived within Rome's imperial frontiers were citizens, but movement towards that final consummation was irregular and without consistent policy.

Julius Caesar was ahead of his contemporaries in his clear desire to extend the civilian status, and Lysias was openly envious of Paul, who by virtue of a grant of citizenship, perhaps by Pompey, to a section of Tarsian Jews, was 'born free'. A Roman colony, which was built and founded as a bulwark of defence in the original conception, had a citizen élite in the founding colonists and their descendants. Philippi, founded to be a bastion of northern Greece, was a case in point, and the anxiety of the *praetors* of that city over their folly in maltreating Paul is manifest. At this time there were over five million citizens in the Roman world. The census of Claudius, held in AD 47, numbers, in fact, 5,984,072 with civic rights.

Originally the citizen had some heavy duties, as well as privileges. Military service was one such obligation which had eroded with the growth of a professional army. The vote was no longer relevant. To be exempt, however, from harsh summary trial and punishment was a real privilege, as was also the right of appeal. Hence the relevance of Lysias' warning to his commander. The word 'Roman' is used in this political sense six times in Acts (16:37,38;22:25-27,29) and the fact shows that the citizenship was becoming a symbol of the Empire's unity. It is fascinating thus to hear a Jew speak, a Hellenistic Jew, containing in his life and life's conduct the three cultures which were fused in Christianity to form Western civilisation. It is not for nothing that we must regard the apostle as the first true European. His citizenship, a badge of dishonour with his nationalist contemporaries, is also a key to our understanding of his evangelism.

Porcius Festus

Festus succeeded to the mismanaged procuratorship of Judea in AD 57 or 58, and the brief episode of his examination of Paul, and the formal consultation with Agrippa II, is another interesting glimpse of a Roman governor at work in a difficult situation. Festus had inherited from Felix a lamentable load of trouble. There was lawlessness in the countryside, and armed rivalry between the factions of the hierarchy. Events were in full flow for the disaster of eight years later, and Festus could not afford to alienate collaborating elements, while the determination of the priests to eliminate an obviously innocent man was a problem which required some careful handling. It was Pilate's situation of thirty years before, repeated with other actors and on another stage. Festus, however, was a luckier man than Pilate. He found a way of escape through the prisoner's own action. He had offered Paul an acquittal on the charge of sedition, and added the proposal, not at all unreasonable from his point of view, that the ex-Pharisee should face a religious investigation before his peers, who were competent, he assumed, to decide a question of heresy.

For Paul it was a crisis. He knew the perils of Jerusalem. He had grasped the realities of the political situation, perhaps for the first time, the growing tension, and the deepening anarchy. He summed it up better than the procurator himself. If Festus found himself inhibited by official policy from refusing and frustrating the Jerusalem hierarchy, Paul proposed to cut the knot for him, to save himself and also to free the governor from all embarrassment by exercising a Roman citizen's right. He appealed to Caesar.

The appeal

The process to which Paul had recourse was the act by which a litigant disputes a judgement, with the consequence that the case is referred to a higher court, normally that of the authority who had originally appointed the magistrate of the court from which the appeal originated. Caesar had appointed Festus. All procurators were imperial appointments. Festus was obliged to accept the appeal, and refer it on, accompanied by the relevant documents and a personal report, which must have presented some difficulty. He saw no fault in Paul by any standards of law and justice familiar to him. He was newly arrived in Palestine, and Jewish law and Jewish religion were both unfamiliar, indeed completely baffling, to him. In his difficult office he was not free to sweep such matters aside with a Gallio's contempt. Festus had his career to make. His difficult province was a hard testing-ground, and the lucidity and correct terminology of a document over his signature in a court so exalted as that of Caesar himself must have been a matter of anxious concern. Hence the alacrity with which he availed himself of the help of Agrippa II.

The Jews had no complaints to level against Festus. He was possibly the best of the procurators. It is a pity that he died two years or thereabouts later.

CHAPTER EIGHT

The Greek World

The Greeks

As universal a fact and a presence in the world to which Christ came was the 'Dispersion of the Greeks'. They were those whose wide migration followed that amazing historical event, Alexander's 'drive to the East'. The Greeks had always been a colonising nation, though not after the fashion of Roman or Anglo-Saxon. The rugged little peninsula of the Greek homeland had limited arable land, and could not, for the most part, support large urban communities. That is how they came to Hellenise Ionia, the blunt end of the Asia Minor peninsula. That is how their colonies, dating from the early centuries of the first millennium before Christ, came to dot the northern coastline of the Mediterranean, the rim of the Black Sea, the Levant, and half of northern Africa.

Their colonies sought no conquest, no penetration of the hinterland. They were thick enough in the lower half of the Italian peninsula for the region to be called Great Greece or Magna Graecia. They were no military problem for Rome, but early in Roman history began their cultural invasion of Rome, that type of spiritual penetration which was part of the Greek genius to transmit.

After Philip the Second of Macedon, whose bones have very recently been found in a rich tomb, had rough-handedly unified a Greece which, for all its political inventiveness, could never unify itself, Alexander, the Macedonian conqueror's son, set out to give a united metropolitan Greece a cause to occupy them – a war of revenge, no less, against Persia, which, a century and a half before, had launched two invasions against Greece. Alexander, like Augustus, is an illustration of the supreme role of personality in history. No one could have foreseen him. A born leader and general, a man, perhaps the first since Abraham, with a global view of his kind, he used his drilled and powerful *phalanx* to cut through the decaying structure of the great Persian Empire. Greek culture followed him. It already had cultural bases, but Alexander promoted Greek migration. When, after his premature death in 323 BC, the conquered east, as far as Kashmir, as we know the area today, was left leaderless, Alexander's armies, and the Greek migrants which with astonishing rapidity followed them, took over the world. It fell into four parts; metropolitan Greece; Syria which, with its capital at Antioch, governed from Asia Minor to the Nile, under Seleucus, one of Alexander's generals; Egypt under Ptolemy, another; and that shadowy kingdom to the east of which we know so little, under the fourth commander, Demetrius.

This, of course, simplifies. Kingdoms like Pergamum carved themselves out of the remoter reaches of Syria. The boundaries between the fiefs of Seleucus and Ptolemy fluctuated up and down Palestine; the kingdom of Demetrius failed to hold its territory for Hellenism, and was reabsorbed into 'the east' after generations, some

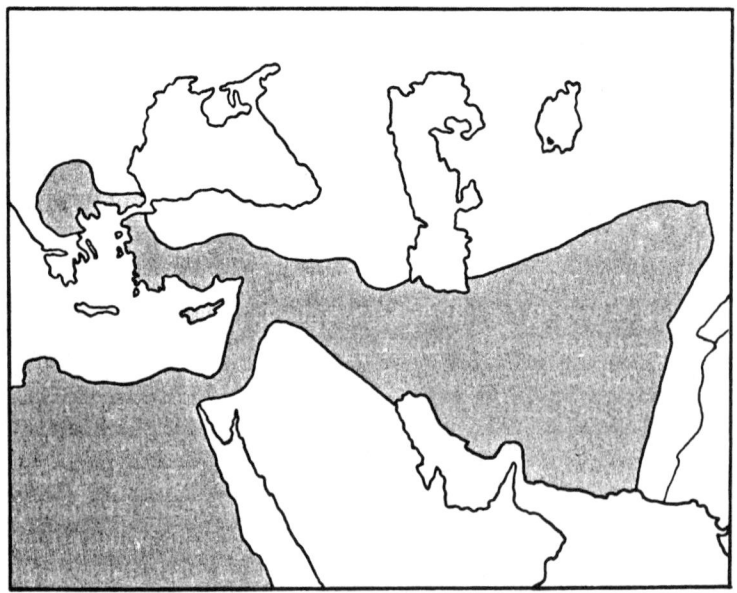

The Greek Empire at its height c.323 BC

picture of which the archaeologists seek to reconstruct from ruins and coins. The fact, however, remains that a great half circle of territory round the eastern end of the Mediterranean remained culturally and politically in Greek hands. Except for the tough and intransigent Jews, the overlordship of the Greeks was accepted.

Greek gave that great swathe of territory a second language and made the New Testament possible. People like Paul and his fellow Jews of the Greek world (John 7:35) became a cultural and historical possibility. Alexandria, a huge city of possibly a million people, fathered a Silver Age of Greek literature. The city was almost half Jewish, and hostility between Jew and Greek was perennial, and provoked a stern letter from the Emperor Claudius in AD 42. It was the Jews of Alexandria, however, who gave the Gentile world the Septuagint, the Greek Bible, so named because of the tradition that it was the work of seventy rabbis.

The effect of the Septuagint was remarkable. It appears from his sermons to have been Peter's Bible, and probably was more widely comprehensible among Aramaic-speaking Jews, who had lost contact with pure classical Hebrew, than their own Scriptures. There is some evidence that Vergil had seen a copy of Isaiah, and thousands of converts must have come to Jewry, because a hungry world found what it sought in their Scriptures. Hence the phenomenon of the Hellenistic Jew – Stephen, Philip and supremely Paul, who could interpret in the forms and context of Greek thought the concepts of the new faith. It is fascinating to see the meeting of the two tides. The Hebrew Dispersion had been going on for centuries, beginning with the Captivity. The movement had been mainly west. The Greek Dispersion had also been going on for three centuries in a wide flood. The preparation for the gospel was on these two fronts.

It will be necessary, in conformity with our theme, to look at two passages in which Jesus and Paul in turn, a score of years apart, made dramatic and illuminating contact with ethnic Greeks, and when we turn to the Jews, a closer look must be taken at the Hellenistic Jews. But a few words must first be said about the use of the word 'Greek' in the New Testament. Curiously enough, the word 'Jew' must be similarly scrutinised by the reader of John's Gospel. But that in its proper place ...

The first use of the word 'Greek' was, of course, as a designation of that volatile and clever race in an ethnic context (John 12:20; Acts 11:20;14:1;16:1;17:4,12;18:4;19:10,17;20:21;21:28; Rom. 1:14, 1 Cor. 1:22,23,24). In Rom. 1:14 Paul uses the ethnic term in a wider sense to mean the civilised as against the uncivilised. The Greeks called those who spoke no Greek *barbaroi* on the sole grounds that their language sounded like *bar bar*. It implied no cultural inferiority, and indeed was used by the Athenians of the fifth century to designate the Persians, whose material civilisation they recognised as superior. A similar word from the same root is also used for expatriate Jews living among the Gentiles, or, who, having thus lived, had returned to live in Jerusalem, for example 'the Grecians' or 'Hellenists' of Acts 6:1 and 9:29, but not, it seems, the 'Grecians' of Acts 11:20 (KJV).

The Jews were well enough aware of the need to live and to function among the Greeks, whose dispersion flowed and eddied with their own. They shrewdly chose Greek names, often by assonance – Paul for Saul, Apelles and Apollos probably for Abel. John Mark bore both a Greek and Hebrew name. Jason may have been Joshua. Timothy had probably only a Greek name, given by his father. Look at the list of those in Rom. 16, members of the church in the capital. There is among them pure Hebrew, Greek and Latin, so completely did the expatriate Jew mingle with the Gentile environment. Horace in 23 BC jokes in a Latin satire about the credulity of 'Judaeus Apelles', 'the Jew Abel'. Juvenal similarly jibes, a century later, and also, in his third satire, provides evidence of a Jewish shanty town outside the Capena Gate at Rome – even using the word *cophinus*, the term used by John for the disciples' Jewish baskets (John 6:13).

The Greeks and Jesus

We shall turn now to the two stories of Greeks in the New Testament, which must obviously be examined. We have opted for the conclusion that the Greeks of John 12:20 were ethnic Greeks probably from the Decapolis. This area stretched north-east to Damascus and south to Amman, the ancient Philadelphia. Jerash, whose great ruins fascinate the tourist today, was one of the ten towns, Gerasa. The area was crowded with Greeks whose immigrant beginnings went back to the conquests of Alexander. Here perhaps was the 'far country' of the Prodigal Son's wanderings. And here Greek confronted Jew, and Jew the alien Greek. It was inevitable that one should influence the other, and since Christ often crossed the lake, it was equally certain that the Greeks should know something of him.

'Sir,' said the visitors to Andrew, 'we want to see Jesus'. Jesus made a curious comment to them. He said: 'Except a corn of wheat fall into the ground and die, it remains simply a corn of wheat. But if it die it brings forth much fruit.'

Hence the relevance of a great slab of carved stone in Athens. It was carved in the fifth century before Christ and depicts the origin of a religious cult dear to the Athenians. It was domiciled at Eleusis, now an industrial suburb of Athens, and thousands of Athenians went through its mystic ritual every year, not, it may be granted, without beneficent influence on the lives of those initiated into the cult. The annual ceremonies were elaborate and laced with emotion, and designed to promote a conviction of spiritual rebirth. Initiates kept a vow of secrecy, but it is known that part of the ceremonial was the uplifting of an ear of wheat. It is interesting to see lying in the grass amid the ruins, which are not tended with the care the Athenians usually bestow on their antiquities, a lintel carved with a sheaf of corn.

Every Greek, including the visitors from the Decapolis, would know the origin of it all. In desperate search for her daughter Kore (The Maiden), Demeter, the Earth Mother, came in grief to Eleusis. Kore had been kidnapped by Pluto, ruler of the Underworld, to be his bride, and in sorrow and anger Demeter sent sterility to the earth until her daughter should be found. The king of Eleusis kindly received the goddess, not knowing, like Abraham, that he entertained a divine being unawares, until strange events in the household made the goddess' presence felt. Demeter remained until Zeus forced a compromise, and Pluto surrendered his bride for six months of each year. Thus it was that winter and summer began their alternation. It is one of the many legends of resurrection which haunt all mythology – a sort of premonition of truth yet to be revealed. A 'dream of the race come true' was how C.S. Lewis related such stories to the historic realities of the faith.

On her departure, Demeter gave 'a corn of wheat' to the little prince Triptolemos, eldest son of Celeus, her royal host. She told him to place it in the ground and expect a fruitful resurrection. So wheat came to bless the fields and tables of men, and since Demeter's Roman name was Ceres, we commemorate the myth with every 'cereal' breakfast food. The large relief in the Athens museum shows the small boy in the act of receiving the grain. It is surely clear that Christ saw in the legend familiar to his foreign visitors a truth about to be illustrated in the historic situation of the Easter story of the death on Calvary and the empty tomb.

It is also odd that when Paul, in AD 52, wrote on death and resurrection to the Christian church in the cosmopolitan port of Corinth – words familiar in a thousand funeral services – he should also speak of the death and transformation in new life of a corn of wheat. He was remembering two things – his route to Corinth from Athens which would pass through Eleusis, and a strangely luminous saying of Christ which was not to be set down for forty years.

It also follows that the saying of Christ must have been known in the early Christian communities, as the doctrine of the rebirth certainly was, long before John, at the end of the century, undertook to write about them.

It was suggested that the visitors came from the Ten Towns, and it merely emphasises the impact that eastern belt of free cities, a phenomenon of the Greek eastern *diaspora* or Dispersion, must have had on the territory of the Jews which lay between them and the Mediterranean. They were all important strong points of the Syrian empire, one of the four 'successor states' of Alexander's mighty empire by the end of the third century before Christ. They seem to have flourished under Rome in whose imperial eyes they were strong points both militarily and culturally, and allies on the precariously policed inner curve of the Fertile Crescent. Pompey, in his efficient organisation of the east in 64, 63 BC, recognised the spirit of the Ten Towns, and, in the words of Josephus, 'restored the cities to their citizens', no doubt in some fiction of an operating democracy in the old Greek tradition. Some of the towns dated their coinage from Pompey, and it is all an arrangement typical of Rome's constant readiness to allow a functioning organisation to function. The towns were caravan cities noisy with trade, and the fact that Bethshan or Scythopolis was one of them, and on the west of Jordan south of the lake, is evidence of the desire to hold such a gateway of trade, and such a door to the Esdraelon Plain. They all commanded roads and drew wealth from trade. The tremendous ruins of Gerasa with its oval forum, its great shopping malls, temples, theatre is a striking relic which has survived.

Across the lake, five to eight miles wide, the fisherfolk and peasants of Galilee could see another, a Gentile world, and it must have exercised a fascination for many liberally-minded Jews, an attraction of which the story of the Prodigal Son is no doubt a striking memorial. It was a 'far country' indeed in culture, ethics, philosophy. Large crowds from the Decapolis followed Christ at the beginning of his ministry (Matt. 4:25). He visited the area when he returned from his one foray outside Israelite territory, his visit to Tyre.

The great geographer, G.A. Smith, is worth quoting:

> We cannot believe that the two worlds, which this landscape embraced, did not break into each other. The many roads which crossed Galilee from the Decapolis to the coast, the many inscriptions upon them, the constant trade between the fishermen and the Greek exporters of their fish, the very coins, thrust Greek upon the Jews of

Galilee. The Aramaic dialect began now to be full of Greek words. It is impossible to believe that our Lord and his disciples did not know Greek. But at least in Gadara, that characteristic Greek city overhanging the Lake of Galilee, and in the scholars it sent forth to Greece and Rome, we have ample proof that the Kingdom of God came forth in no obscure corner, but in the very face of the kingdoms of this world.

Paul and the Athenians

It was only twenty years later that Paul came to Athens, the cultural centre of the world, and provided literature and history with a remarkable glimpse of life in that historic city, which was the scene of such triumphs of art and literature over the half century of her Golden Age, as no other place or time has shown.

Luke wrote the story, and the narrative contains the compact outline of a speech made by the writer's friend, Paul, before the Court of the Areopagus. It may be read today, in exquisite Greek lettering, on an oblong bronze plaque set in the rocky face of the worn outcrop of stone beneath the commanding mass of the Acropolis. The Athenians called the rock mound the Hill of Ares, or the Areopagus.

The story is found in the seventeenth chapter of the Acts of the Apostles, and forms, for any classical historian, a most remarkable passage. Simply translated, it runs:

> While Paul was waiting for his friends in Athens, he was deeply stirred to see the city given over to idols. And so in the synagogue he debated with the Jews and their adherents, and in the market-place every day with any he chanced to meet. Some of the Epicurean and Stoic philosophers met him, and some of them said: 'What is the purpose of this picker-up of oddments?' And others said: 'He appears to be a preacher of foreign deities' – for Paul was preaching the gospel of Jesus and the resurrection. So they brought him urgently to the Hill of Ares, saying: 'May we know this new teaching of which you speak? For you bring to our hearing matters quite strange to us. And so we want to know what these things mean.' (All the Athenians and the strangers residing there spent their leisure in nothing else but talking and hearing about something new.) ... Paul stood in the middle of the Hill of Ares and said: 'Athenians, I observe that in every way you are uncommonly religious, for going about and looking at the objects of your worship, I even found an altar on which was inscribed TO THE UNKNOWN GOD! That which you worship, therefore, in ignorance, I am making known to you. God who made the universe and all that it contains, he, the Lord from all time of the heavens and the earth, does not dwell in temples which hands have made, nor is he served by human hands, as though he needed something, giving, as he does to all, life, and breath, and everything. And he made of one blood every race of men, causing them to dwell upon all the face of the earth,

marking out for them their boundaries in time, and their place of habitation, and prompting them to seek God, if perhaps they might grope for him, and discover him, though indeed he is not far from any one of us. For in him we live, and move, and indeed, exist, as some of your own Stoic poets have said: 'For we are also his offspring.' Being therefore, by the nature of things, God's offspring, we ought not to think that the Divine is like gold, or silver, or stone, carved work of man's devising. Well, then, the times of ignorance God overlooked, but now calls on all men everywhere to repent because he has set a day in which he purposes to judge the world in righteousness, by the Man whom he has appointed, giving assurance to all men by raising him from the dead.' Having heard of a resurrection of the dead, some scoffed. Others said: 'We shall hear you again about this.' So Paul came out from their company. But some men remained with him and believed. Among whom was Dionysius a member of the Court of the Hill of Ares, a woman named Damaris, and others along with them.

The circumstances merit an effort of the imagination. Paul had come alone to the great city, somewhat troubled and anxious. Northern Greece, his first encounter with Europe, had seen stormy experience, and in Athens, suffering some reaction, Paul was a prey to that sharp loneliness felt by sensitive spirits amid an alien throng, and in an environment which disturbs and repels. And it seems clear that Athens did appear to Paul of Tarsus, for all his deep understanding of the Greeks, a hostile and uncongenial place in the summer of AD 50.

The reasons are not far to seek. Those who view with wonder the magnificence of Athens' ruined heart today are without the Jew's deep loathing of idolatry. The modern visitor who climbs the steps through the Propylaea, and sees the breath-taking majesty of the shattered Parthenon, mellow in its golden marble, superbly placed, has no thought of Athene, who once stood in the dim interior, the object of man's devotion. He may trace the base of another colossal image of Athens' patron goddess in the precinct. It stood with spear upraised so high that sailors off Sunion caught the sun's glint on its point from forty miles away. When the Goths intruded at the beginning of the dark fifth century after Christ, they scattered in flight at the first sight of the image. The modern visitor standing on the flat foundation regrets the destruction of a great statue. The reverence of the Athenian, the terror of the Goth, the repugnance of the Jew for blasphemy in bronze and stone, mean nothing to him.

Perhaps the Christian can still touch the edge of that deep sensation only in the revolting presence of the phallic image. Some fragments, vast and intricately carved on Delos, reveal the gross mingling of carnality and religion which stirred the wrath of the

The Acropolis at Athens

Hebrew prophets, and which evoke a Christian disgust. The sculptured sensualities of some Eastern temples stir the same nausea. Athens must have had examples enough of this baser use of Greek art. Athene Promachos and the Wingless Victory were not its only creations. Idolatry was real and obtrusive, a matter of disgust for Paul.

Another reason for Paul's disturbance of spirit is more elusive. Perhaps he caught the atmosphere of Athens' decadence. There is no exhilaration in the twilight of a great culture. Luke, often a master of brief irony, felt the shallow artificiality of the place. 'All the Athenians, and strangers residing there,' he wrote, 'spent their leisure in nothing else but talking and hearing about something new.' To this cult of curiosity the old Greek sense of wonder had deteriorated. Even in the great creative days, Athenian curiosity had shown its shabbier side in a manner which infuriated orators as diverse as the crude Cleon and the patriot Demosthenes. 'You are spectators in displays of oratory,' shouted the former in 427 BC, 'and listeners to the tales of others' doings.' Half a century later, the great Demosthenes, striving in vain to awaken a declining people to the menace of that oddly Hitler-like person, Philip the Second of Macedon, asked ironically: 'Do you like walking about and asking one another: Is there any news? Why, could there be greater news than a man of Macedon subduing Athenians, and directing the affairs of Greece?' 'Is there any news?' Demosthenes' adjective is the very one used by Luke in the comment quoted – 'some new thing'.

The great orator's scorn was four centuries old when Paul came to Athens. Decadence, indeed, had been sharp and swift from the high days of the fifth century. The fearful tension of the Thirty Years' War with Sparta which closed the Golden Age, whose effects were so terribly diagnosed by Thucydides, was the major cause of decline. The judicial murder of Socrates was one of the first symptoms. Plato's stern authoritarianism was a reaction. So were the philosophies of escape and resistance of a century later, the doctrines of Epicurus and the Stoics.

Strangely, however, the city still lived on the brief glory of the astonishing fifth century. Athens does still. The modern student peoples the *agora* (market place) with the Greeks of Pericles, not with those of Luke, or even of Epicurus and Demosthenes. The voice of that short noontide of confidence, achievement, and endeavour comes too loud and clear. The Parthenon, and the fragments of the magnificence which surrounded it, set proudly on the incomparable platform of the Acropolis, still speak in lasting stone of a generation aflame with the memory of a mighty victory over mortal peril from Asia, of a people which saw nothing too difficult for their creating. Pen, too, vied with chisel to create memorials of a burst of high endeavour which left a mark on history, for a Golden Age is inevitably one when artist and people know no division, when literature is a nation's voice, and art its truest awareness.

The Golden Age had no afternoon. 'Men build their empire', writes D.L. Page, 'out of poverty and hardship; then rest awhile to enjoy their comfort and security; later, since peace and plenty breed satiety, a generation which has not toiled demands response no longer, convention and comfort recreate the restless and the critical, decline or change comes quickly. The tragic difference of Athens was that she omitted the intermediate phase. She climbed to the peak of her mountain and rushed straight down without stopping to enjoy the prospect. Athens had no Victorian age.' Its achievements, to be sure, lived on to daunt and to inspire, while its taste, its thought, its spirit found some form of interpretation and expression in the Hellenism which spread through the world in Alexander's wake, and coloured the thinking of men like Stephen and Paul. The world at large recognised all this. Hence the amazing success with which another Athens lived on its vanished past. Conquerors spared it for no other reason. Under Rome Athens was a 'free city', and this was more than 'the contemptuous boon of an unfettered loquacity', as

Dean Farrar put it in a purple passage. Hadrian's adornment of the city reveals the genuine love and admiration her reputation could still inspire in men of another race. 'Captive Greece', as Horace put it, could still 'take captive her fierce conqueror'.

Of 'unfettered loquacity' there was, of course, enough and to spare, and any reincarnated Aristophanes, abroad in a modern university city, or indeed in the church, might make a sardonic retort. But Paul had small regard for such shallow culture. His sturdy faith could be pungently contemptuous of aimless philosophies. His shrewd mind must have noted the speculation for speculation's sake, and the glib talk for the sake of talking, the old vice of sophistry which Aristophanes and Plato had flayed, turned then, as never before, cynically to profit. He must have observed the commercialisation of knowledge and culture, the horde who lived by wits and words, in short, all the sham, the artificiality, the dishonesty, and empty pride of a city living on its past, its ghosts, and its relics. The encounter was no joyous experience to a Jew of Tarsus ardent for truth.

It was disturbing, too, to be taken for yet another fortune-seeker, eager to sell his doctrine. 'What,' they asked, observing his Socratic activities in the *agora*, 'does this "seed-picker" want?' The word was Athenian slang. It was used by Aristophanes in his uproarious comedy *The Birds* to signify the busy winged things of the meadows, snapping up the chance fallen seed, the pert sparrows and finches of the furrows. In Athenian vernacular it came to mean the sophistic picker-up of scraps of learning, the liver on his words and wits, a 'babbler' only in the sense that such charlatans were compelled to talk long and persuasively to conceal the second-hand, second-rate quality of their doctrine. The word is an authentic echo of the crowded *agora*, where Paul, conforming easily to Athenian tradition as old as Socrates, met the inquisitive quick-tongued populace, joined in the animated discussion which was the habit and manner of their market-place, and attracted the attention of the Stoics and Epicureans.

Hence a polite summons to appear before the Court of Areopagus, which the philosophers of both schools seem to have controlled. They were rivals for the attention of their day, for the Greeks lacked somewhat the Roman penchant for eclecticism which enabled urbane folk like Horace to be Stoic and Epicurean at one and the same time. Within a mile of the *agora* were the Gardens of Epicurus. The *Stoa Poikile*, from which the Stoics took their name, closed the end of the market-place. Paul was in the ancient centre and capital city of both philosophies, four centuries after their first foundation.

At Athens both were professed with academic exclusiveness.

Both Epicureanism and Stoicism had been the response of a stricken generation to a world grown harsh and hostile with the passing of an era. Zeno of Citium, founder of the Stoic school, lived from 340 to 260 BC. Epicurus' dates almost exactly coincide. They are 342 to 270 BC. It was, in Toynbee's phrase, the Hellenic 'Time of Troubles.' The Greek states had become the protectorates of Macedon. Liberty, abused everywhere when the city-states enjoyed it, was lost under foreign autocracy. Unity, elusive or scorned when it could have been found by free-will and a common purpose, had been imposed rough-handedly by the half-barbarous kingdom of the north. Stoicism and Epicureanism were a spiritual reaction and response. Each in its own way, the two systems sought to fortify souls in torment at the spectacle of political breakdown, and provide code and dogma in a sombre age of tension.

The Stoics and Epicureans

To understand Paul's address it is necessary to look a little more closely at the two philosophic systems followed by his audience. It must have been about the year 320 BC when Epicurus, the son of a schoolmaster of Samos, discovered the atomic theory of Democritus of Abdera. Atoms, Democritus taught, small indivisible particles variously shaped, form the universe. Plunging through the void with velocities proportioned to their size, these fundamental particles clash with one another forming, in this fashion, coherent groups. The world and all that is in it is thus made. Chance alone rules, and infinite time, with the infinite variations, congregation, and cohesion of the basic material, has produced things animate and inanimate.

It was materialism thorough and absolute. The soul and mind, according to Democritus, was atomic in structure, atoms round and mobile, and infinitely subtle. Sight, hearing, taste, were the impinging of atoms on the senses, themselves material in composition and structure. Hence, in the midst of a virtual atheism, Epicurus' need to admit the existence of deities. In dreams and visions of the night such beings became part of human consciousness, and, caught by his own system, Epicurus could only explain such mental phenomena by his theory of vision. Films of atoms, given off by tangible realities, however subtle, formed the stuff of dreams.

But he denied that such contacts with another order of being implied a theology of involvement. The gods cared nothing for man. As Tennyson puts it in the choric song of *The Lotus Eaters*,

> ... *they lie beside their nectar, and the bolts are hurl'd*
> *Far below them in the valleys, and the clouds are lightly curl'd*
> *Round their golden houses, girdled with the gleaming world:*
> *Where they smile in secret, looking over wasted lands,*
> *Blight and famine, plague and earthquake, roaring deeps and fiery sands,*
> *Clanging fights, and flaming towns, and sinking ships, and praying hands.*
> *But they smile, they find a music centred in a doleful song*
> *Steaming up, a lamentation and an ancient tale of wrong ...*

Behind such physical doctrine lay Epicurus' passionate quest for peace of mind. He saw religion, the hope or fear of survival, the expectation of judgement, a power which punished, cared or interfered, as disturbance for the soul, and a poison of its peace. Let man seek only happiness; and happiness, in a world so material, could only be pleasure.

Hence the inevitable betrayal of Epicurus by human nature. The word 'epicurean' suggests to modern ears a selfish seeker after creature comfort. An 'epicure' is, in its better meaning, one who cultivates a fine taste at the table; at its nether end, a mere glutton. The elegant Petronius, or the Horace of more than one ode, are, to the casual student of antiquity, the 'epicureans' of the past rather than the good master himself, who was something of a saint, and far from carnal. For such misunderstanding the system must bear its share of blame. Pleasure is too subjective a word, too charged with the experience of sense, easily to bear a philosophic meaning.

Epicureanism was, therefore, rapidly corrupted by those who sought a philosophic cloak for self-indulgence. The speech of Cicero against Piso, an oration which, in point of fact, does the great orator little credit, contains a good illustration. A Greek told Piso of a philosophy which enthroned pleasure as the highest good. 'A truly dangerous word', says Cicero, 'for a young man not notable for his intelligence'; Piso laid hold of such information avidly. 'He neighed at the word,' says Cicero. The Greek tried to explain what Epicurus meant by pleasure, but Piso had his dogma and was in no mood to have it watered down, and as for the Greek, who was he to differ too vehemently from a magistrate of Rome?

Such misapprehension was inevitable. The shrewd Roman Fabricius saw its significance while Epicurus was still alive. The story goes that Pyrrhus' ambassador told the Romans of the philosopher in

282 BC, and the Roman consul displayed a shrewd knowledge of human nature when he expressed the hope that Epicurus would win many converts among the Samnites, indeed among all the enemies of Rome. The yoke in fact was too easy, but this is the limit of Epicurus' blame. The master, rightly understood, exalted virtue as true pleasure's prerequisite, and pointed the way to peace, not debauchery. Seneca, who had no brief for him, wrote: 'I dare to state, in the face of the opinions of some, that the ethics of Epicurus are sane, upright, even austere, for the man who penetrates their depth.'

The true sage, Epicurus taught, curbed passion, scorned excess, lust, ambition, for all have aftermath of pain. He narrowed desire, that disappointment, anxiety, apprehension, desire's by-products, might not ruffle his calm and sought health, quietness, simplicity, for all are part of the unseen, unenvied way. He pursued, in short, a species of quietism, without much doctrine save the view of physics on which so much depended, and without mystery or complication. Virile souls may have turned more readily to Stoicism. The timid of a disillusioned age found more obvious escape in Epicureanism.

There is no means of knowing the colour or temper of the Epicureanism held by the philosophers of Paul's audience. They were academic types, sound, no doubt, in doctrine, virtual atheists in consequence, contemptuous of all belief in divine care for human virtue, human sin, or human life at large. Josephus, who described the Epicureans as the Sadducees of the Athenian philosophic world, probably touched the truth. The worldly Jewish sect, holding doctrine lightly, and denying another life, the resurrection and the judgement, were not dissimilar in outlook. Significantly, Paul disregarded both groups in two notable addresses. It is idle to speak to those with whom there is no point of contact, no overlap of experience. Paul chose to speak rather to the Pharisees in Jerusalem, and to the Stoics of his Athenian audience. Those committed to Epicurus, or to what men had made of Epicurus, were not open to his argument.

Paul must have known much of Stoicism. Zeno, the founder of the school, came from Paul's corner of the Mediterranean, Citium in Cyprus. A second Zeno, who was head of the school in 204 BC, actually came from Tarsus. He it was who gave Stoicism the practical turn which so attracted the intelligent Roman. Aratus, scientist and poet, who is quoted by Paul in the speech before the Areopagus, was a Stoic of the first vintage, born at Soli in Cilicia, and converted to Stoicism a few yards from where Paul spoke. Cleanthes, whose hymn to Zeus also uses the words of Paul's quotation, was a man of Assos in Asia Minor. As second head of the school, he infused a deeply religious element into Stoicism.

Zeno, first founder of the Stoic school, and it appears, a Semite, came to Athens about the year 320 BC, at the very time when Epicurus was finding delight and relief in the atomic theory of Democritus in Colophon across the Aegean. Two questions confronted Zeno, as they confront all seekers after truth — what to believe, and how to live. Those questions have never been dissociated. It has already been shown how Epicurus answered them, and the heresy which emerged. Zeno's answers were more noble and exacting.

Nothing but goodness is good, he averred. Rank, riches, health, race, pleasure are incidentals. Epicurus might argue that pleasure is good, and find the bulk of the world to support him. But does history ever praise a man because he was happy, healthy, long-lived, or rich? No. What lives in memory is a man's goodness, virtue, heroism. The verdict of history is obviously groping after some form of ultimate justice. A man, therefore, if he but realises, possesses all good in his person. What matters is what he is, not what he has or what happens to him. No earthly power can make a man bad outside his own will. It can rob him of freedom, health, possessions but not of goodness. Why then fear, when, fundamentally, a man is free, safe, inviolate?

And what is goodness? A good day, a good knife, a good ship is one which fulfils its proper function well. A good man is one who fulfils his human function well. And what do we mean by 'well'? To answer this question Stoicism pointed to the conception of *phusis*, 'the process of growth' if one may hazard a translation. All things visible are moving to an end, a perfection, the seed towards the plant, the young to adulthood, the disorganised society towards the city-state. *Phusis* is the force which promotes the process, a thrust, a drive towards the complete, the good. To live well, then, is to live 'according to *phusis*', in alliance, that is, and conformity with the great life force which pervades like a soul all Creation, making a *cosmos*, or an order out of it, and infusing it all with purpose.

From this concept emerged the Stoic conception of God, hardly a personal God, but not unlike the 'Ultimate Reality' imagined by some post-Christian theologians. It is pantheism in a broad sense, because if God is *phusis*, and *phusis* cannot be understood or conceived apart from that which it indwells and interfuses, so God is Everything. The universe is a living whole, filled and animated by one soul. But if to live 'according to *phusis*' is to fulfil 'the will of God', how, the objection arises, can anyone do other than the will of God, if God is all? The Stoic avoided this Calvinist dilemma by answering that God is indeed in all, save in the doings of bad men, for man is free. Man's soul is part of the divine fire, and so partakes of the freedom of God himself. Men can co-operate or rebel, though rebellion, in the nature of things, spells disaster. At this point a personal God is perilously near emerging, and no doubt in their human variety of religious experience many a Stoic thought of communion with God in deeply personal terms.

A way of life manifestly follows. The Labours of Hercules become a Stoic myth for the toilsome living of a servant of mankind. Stoic Emperors like Trajan, Hadrian, and above all Marcus Aurelius, who toiled for the Empire, were practical exponents of this aspect of Stoicism. The other feature of Stoicism, its scorn of all earthly things apart from goodness, produced that taut defiance of the world, that tight-lipped endurance and stubborn withdrawal which marked the Stoic opposition under the early Caesars, and which was a feature of Paul's contemporary Rome. In short, Stoicism gave men armour in an evil day, and in days of good it urged them on. If its corruption was a philosophic Pharisaism, that was not the fault of the system.

It is easy to see why Paul addressed himself to the Stoics of his audience. He, too, believed in a purpose working to a vast consummation, and the need for man to co-operate with it. He, too, believed that what a man was mattered supremely, and not what he possessed. He, too, sought self-sufficiency and superiority to circumstances. His God, too, was, in Paul's view, transcendent, and beyond the patronage of man. There were points of sympathy and contact, a bridgehead of persuasion.

The address itself must now be considered. The approach was conciliatory and courteous, but perhaps just touched with that irony which was the common fashion of Athenian speech. 'Athenians', said Paul, 'I observe that in every way you are uncommonly religious.' Here was Athenian *parrhesia* (free speech) of the first order, tactful yet challenging, polite yet without sacrifice of the speaker's position. 'As I have moved about your city looking at the objects of your worship', Paul continued, 'I came upon an altar inscribed TO THE UNKNOWN GOD.' Thus it must be translated. In the Greek there is noun and adjective only, without either a definite or indefinite article. One or two examples of such inscriptions survive, but always in the plural, TO UNKNOWN GODS. In the plural, English can avoid a choice. In the singular, choice must be made between the definite and indefinite article. The definite is better, provided the reference and context of the inscription are realised. The inscription in each case refers to the unknown deity concerned with the altar's foundation, not generally or transcendentally to a God vaguely realised and sought. Paul adapted the inscription for homiletic ends. He was not deceived about its meaning, but like any perceptive preacher sought an illustration and a point of contact in a known environment. The device captured attention and anchored the theme in experience.

What did the inscription mean? Plato preserves a tradition that Epimenides, the Cretan religious teacher and miracle-worker, was in Athens about 500 BC. Some said it was 600 BC, but dates are neither here nor there in a half-legendary situation. The story was that, to combat an epidemic, Epimenides directed the Athenians to loose sheep from the Areopagus, and wherever they lay down to build an altar 'to the unknown god' of the place, and to make sacrifice. Perhaps the story is a tale invented to explain a visible phenomenon. Perhaps the altars merely represented a scrupulosity which, in a city full of deities from all the Eastern Mediterranean, sought to avoid offence to any in this slightly naïve fashion. It is impossible to say more.

It was convenient, however, to Paul's approach, and simple for him to slide from the altar's dedication to the Stoic God who needed nothing from any man. Or was it quite the Stoic God? Not perhaps in the more austere significance of their belief. Paul's Creator was still his own personal God, the great I AM. Indeed he snatches a remembered phrase from a speech which had burned its memory on his brain. It was Stephen, on trial before the Sanhedrin, who had protested in Paul's hearing that 'God does not dwell in temples made with hands'.

Stephen spoke of Solomon's shrine. Paul quoted the words under the great stone altar of Greece, the Acropolis. Whether he spoke on the traditional site, the lower outcrop of stone below the greater, called the Areopagus or the Hill of Ares, or whether the hearing took place in the Royal Porch in the *agora,* as others contend, the magnificence of the temples on the height was in full view, the glorious Parthenon, the Erechtheum, and the fairy-light little shrine of the Wingless Victory on its promontory beside the entrance portal. And wherever he deprecated the thought that deity could be set forth in 'gold, silver or stone, carved work of man's devising', the commanding statue of Athene Promachus lifted its bright-tipped spear above him, and the gold and ivory figure of the same Athene listened from the religious light of her sanctuary in the great temple.

Here, indeed, was a mingling of Hebrew notions of deity and Greek, with the Stoic listeners intent, recognising features of their own belief, but sensing something more personal, more urgently involved in the concept their visitor's words were weaving. It was a touch of the pleader's art to quote Cleanthes' hymn to Zeus. The passage, drastically abbreviated, runs:

> Thou, Zeus, art praised above all gods; many are thy names and thine is the power eternally. The origin of the world was from thee: and by law thou rulest over all things. Unto thee may all flesh speak, *for we are thy offspring*. Therefore will I raise a hymn unto thee: and will ever sing of thy might. The whole order of the heavens obeys thy word, as it moves round the earth, small and great luminaries commingled. How great thou art ...

Aratus of Soli, Paul's Cilician countryman, almost a contemporary of Cleanthes, had also used the words. Notice that Paul says 'poets', plural. This sage wrote a poem called *Phaenomena*, a dull piece, translated by Cicero, and in concept something like Thomson's *Seasons*. Its opening lines run:

> From Zeus let us begin; him do we mortals never leave unnamed; full of Zeus are all the streets and all the market-places of men; full is the sea and the heavens thereof; always we all have need of Zeus. *For we are also his offspring*; and he in his kindness unto men giveth favourable signs and wakeneth the people to work, reminding them of livelihood ...

The indefatigable tracers of quotation suggest that both Cleanthes and Aratus were quoting the phrase 'in him we live' from Epimenides, the Cretan already mentioned for his activities in Athens, and from whom Paul quoted an uncomplimentary line against the Cretans in his letter to Titus. No one can be sure. What is significant is Paul's easy use of popular quotation.

Note that he was grappling with the thought of mankind's unity before God which had been his theme of bitter controversy with the Jews. It is a mark of the greatness of his mind that he could contest the same point in another context, in another framework of thought. It was the boast of the Athenians that they had 'sprung from the soil', and though men of Stoic colouring or conviction, like Seneca and Epictetus, had glimpsed the thought of mankind's unity, it was left to Paul, in two racial and religious settings, to give the concept lifting power and application.

Towards God, says Paul, mankind had ever 'groped'. The word he uses would raise echoes in every listening Greek. Homer and Plato were familiar reading, and every educated man would remember that the verb is used in the *Odyssey* to describe the blinded Cyclops groping for the entrance of his cave, and in the *Phaedo*, Plato's most moving dialogue, for the very search for truth which Paul here envisages on its highest plane, the quest for God. The word, it is true, is used three times in the Septuagint, always for groping in the dark, but Paul must have had familiar Greek contexts in his mind. His easy allusiveness is the impressive point.

So far, so good. With astonishing intellectual dexterity, the Jew of Tarsus, the Pharisee of Gamaliel's school, met the cream of Athens' intelligentsia on their familiar ground, discerned shrewdly the portion of the audience open to his argument, and, with polished persuasion, in their common speech, put his concept of God before them. With fine audacity he swept the Acropolis of its divine significance, dismissing the magnificence of the grandest Greek art as irrelevant in the search for God. It is Athenian free speech at its boldest, exercised and also tolerated, for the broad-minded acceptance of Paul's argument is as remarkable as his courageous use of it. He spoke appropriately to time and place, and couched his message, as the church is ever urged, and rightly urged to do, in the thought-forms of the day.

There are those today who profess a search for an elusive God, greater and higher than 'the God of revelation', and who end bewildered with something not unlike the Stoic *phusis*, some ancient pantheism dressed in modern words, an impersonal or scarcely personal Force, created in the image of Tillich and de Chardin. Paul made no such disastrous mistake, and sought no easy compromise. He met his audience where he could, sought by all means to graft his teaching on to accepted ideas, and to express it in acceptable and comprehensible terms. But he knew that a point of challenge had to come. It came with his introduction of Christ, and the divine authentication of his Person. In the act he lost the bulk of his audience. The Epicureans had listened impatiently throughout. They were those who scoffed. The Stoics dismissed him with more polite formality. The true Stoic, the Wise Man of their famous concept, needed no repentance, feared no day of judgement, looked for no resurrection or reward.

The audience dispersed. If the function of the Areopagus was the informal or formal investigation of new teachings, they no doubt regarded their function as fulfilled. The newcomer had nothing pernicious to disseminate, only the stock-in-trade of the religious enthusiast the world over, and Athens could absorb such trivialities and survive. One member only of the court crossed the Rubicon, and some of the bystanders, for there was no doubt a listening circle. There normally was on such occasions. Round the Acropolis in modern Athens runs the Street of Dionysius the Areopagite. Paul's convert would have been amazed.

A question of some importance remains. From Athens Paul moved on to Corinth, the cosmopolitan city of two seas. Writing some four years later to the contentious church which he founded there, he remarked upon the studied simplicity of the gospel he had preached among them. Are those right who see in this attitude a repudiation of the intellectual approach which marked the Areopagus address? By no means, even if it be correctly assumed that the argument before the philosophers was commonly pursued in the *agora*, a reasonable assumption if the sermon at Lystra is evidence. There, too, Paul had a Gentile audience, unversed in Judaism or Old Testament imagery.

The remark to the Corinthians must be seen in the context of the restrained irony which characterises the first four chapters of the epistle. With the shallow intellectualism of the Corinthians Paul was disposed to waste no time. He was not prepared to give them a Christianity diluted with their pseudo-philosophical ideas, or necessarily expressed in their weakened terminology. Nor had he been prepared to do that in Athens, as the final confrontation of his address amply demonstrates. His talk was not a failure. Dionysius was a triumph, which any intellectual of Christian conviction might envy among his peers. The whole address remains a model for those who seek in such circles to present the Christian faith, and a warning to those who, in misguided moments, have seen a virtue in crudity, and a loyalty to truth in a disrespect for the views, the habits of thought, and the attitudes of intelligent people who fail in all points to follow them. Confrontation there must be, if the popular word may be used again, but with preamble of courtesy, with the tolerance which is not incompatible with earnestness, and with the sincerest of efforts to see good where good has found a place. But what Paul was to call 'the offence of the cross' remains.

What a remarkable story, however, and with what avid interest it would have been seized upon had it emerged today as a newly discovered page of first-century literature. Here was a Hellenistic Jew, moving quietly into the old home of the motherland of Hellenism, a Jew, meeting the intellectuals of the cultured world on their own familiar ground, and doing at length what the Lord had done in brief with quiet dexterity in his meeting with the Greeks.

Hellenism fused with Judaism to produce the New Testament and its theology. In this scene from Athens it is seen at the moment of birth. It was about to begin, in the common dialect, that universal basic Greek which had descended from the delicate, powerful speech of the Classical Greek of Athens' great age, to bring the message of Christianity to the world.

Chapter Nine

The Jewish World

The Jews

Jesus was a Jew, and it will be necessary to look into the variant meanings of that word. It occasions something of the same semantic problems as the word 'Greek' in New Testament contexts, and the reader must be alert for variant shades of meaning.

Primarily a Jew was a member of the tribe of Judah, and references such as 2 Kings 25:25; Neh. 5:8; and Jer. 38:19 seem to establish that use. Even in Jeremiah's day, however, after the fall of the northern kingdom, the word seems to have assumed the wider significance of 'Hebrew'. Jer. 34:9 is quite clear. The Assyrians used the word in this way. Certainly 'Jewish' for 'Hebrew' in general is used in 2 Kings 18:26 and the parallel Isa. 36:11. (See also Neh. 13:24.) By the eighth century BC, therefore, with the decimation and deportation of the northern tribes, 'Jews' were Israelites.

Judas Maccabeus, making contact with Rome in 145 BC, speaks of 'the nation of the Jews' (1 Macc. 8:23,25,27). So, too, throughout Josephus, who wrote between AD 75 and 95. This historian, whose credibility, it might be remarked, grows with widening research and discovery, keeps the term 'Hebrew' for more ancient history than the period between 100 BC and AD 100 for which he is the prime source.

The religious flavour of the word 'Jew' grew from the peculiarity of the race among the Gentiles. It is a fair guess that, around about AD 43, an observant official of Antioch noted a schism among the Jews and listed the dissidents as 'Christians'. The fact implies a very clear appreciation of the religious distinctiveness of the Antiochene Jews (Acts 11:26). The Jews were eager to retain, rather than to blur, the marks of difference. Paul does not call himself a Roman citizen of Tarsus, but 'a Jew of Tarsus', adding a phrase which Euripides had used of Athens, 'a citizen of no mean city.' And it was to a religious group, rather than to an ethnic group, that Julius Caesar granted citizenship: the Jews of Alexandria. They comprised, astonishingly, a third of the population of that great city.

In the Gospels 'the Jews' often denotes the religious leaders of Jerusalem, a term used by the Galilean John, almost with a touch of hostility (John 20:19), as the word 'Yankee' can be used south of the Potomac today, where the Confederate flag is still flown.

Paul pleaded for a deepening of the religious significance of the word at the expense of the ethnic (Rom. 2:17-29). Indeed both Paul and John would deny the name 'Jew' to those who rejected the Messiah (Rom. 9:6; Rev. 2:9). To live 'Jewishly' was the test (Gal. 2:14;3:29).

Jesus then was a Jew in the true ethnic sense of the word, though the whole manner of his life prompted the widening of the term, just as Jews could be Romans by virtue of the gift of citizenship, and Greeks in culture. The three ingredients of the Mediterranean heritage significantly fuse.

The Lord, however, grew up in the circle of the synagogue. He learned letters there in boyhood. He ministered there while permitted to do so. He conformed to the Law when it was the true Law of Moses, and not a fetish of rabbinical commentators (Matt. 5:17;8:4; Mark 2:23-28;3:1-5). Nor did he scorn all custom. The Talmud, for example, directs: 'One should not comfort the mourner while his dead lies before him.' Friends were bidden visit immediately after the burial and through the first week, and to help with comfort and material aid. Observe how strikingly this conforms to the events after Lazarus' death (John 11 – observe, incidentally, in this passage 'the Jews' used as a Galilean might use the term).

The Synagogues

The Lord's ministry was confined almost completely to 'the lost sheep of the children of Israel'. His contacts with Gentiles were minimal, though cordial and without racial discrimination. The remark in Tyre (Matt. 15:21-28; Mark 7:24-30) was ironical, and reflects Christ's rejection of his disciples' murmuring, endured by him all through their walk over the hills from Galilee into the Gentile territory of Tyre. The quick-witted woman immediately caught his meaning and the implied rebuke.

It is with the birth and spread of the church that the preparation for the gospel through the synagogues becomes strikingly visible, along with evidence for the unity and coherence of global Jewry. Global Jewry and its gifts made it possible to implant a global Christianity in a generation. Such diffusion through the Greek and Roman world was the work of the Hellenistic Jews, as the early chapters of Acts so clearly demonstrate. In fusing on several fronts with the Greek Dispersion, the Jewish Dispersion had in no way lost its uncontaminated Jewish heritage. Observe that little cameo of international evangelism where Philip, a Greek Jew, explains Isaiah to an Ethiopian courtier and baptises him (Acts 8:27-38). It is clear that the synagogue had reached Ethiopia, and won Gentile adherents.

Evidence is scanty in a tract of history in which Greek and Roman documents are singularly lacking, but there were Jews in Rome from the middle of the first century before Christ, inspiring the petty kind of hostility which that dauntless race has so often provoked in Gentile territory. The poet Horace, whose chatty poem on a journey to Brundisium in the suite of Augustus' special envoy, Maecenas, has already been mentioned, has a sneer for a Jew named Apella. The man, he says, would believe any superstition. That was about 37 or 38 BC. Curiously enough, it was about that time that Vergil was writing his Tenth Eclogue, a poem in many ways peculiarly different from those which accompanied it. It has been suggested (by Sir William Ramsay, classicist and archaeologist) that its peculiarities could have been inspired by an attempt to imitate the form and content of Isaiah. Had the Greek Septuagint been read by that bilingual poet? The Greek Old Testament had been given to the world for no other reason than to make the Gentiles aware of the Jewish heritage.

A hundred years after this time the bitter satirist, Juvenal, was writing with scorn and contempt of the Jews, whose poorer minority huddled in a shanty town outside the Capena Gate. He pictures, in his horribly modern satire on Rome, a drunken bully yelling at a cornered victim in a slum street at night: 'What prayer-place are you sneaking back from?' The reference was to some synagogue of Roman Jews.

They were all over the world. A cache of papyri, historically most valuable, tells of a temple, rather than a synagogue, which Jews of Nehemiah's day sought to operate at Elephantine, deep down the Nile Valley, at Aswan. They were no doubt a surviving remnant of Jeremiah's dispersion. We have the lintel, or part of it, of the

Corinthian synagogue, and the story of Gallio is evidence enough of the precarious existence such Jewish ghetto minorities endured throughout the Gentile world. Archaeological evidence for the synagogues is, of course, much more widely spread than this.

The remarkable institution goes back to the Babylonian exile. Cut off from their Temple and its elaborate worship, and inhibited from establishing any form of ritual like it elsewhere, the Jews of the Dispersion instinctively sought unity and coherence by gathering together. It might be in houses when conditions eased and remnants of Jewry integrated to some extent with the communities in which they were dispersed. There is some evidence that, failing a building, the Jews gathered by a river. In Psalm 137 we have a tiny piece of drama. Gathered for prayer by the willow-lined Euphrates, the Jews in Babylon find themselves menaced by a hostile pagan crowd, and saved their lives only by a commination, a grim verbal weapon which would strike dread into a superstitious rout of bullying pagans and cause them to retreat.

In Philippi, Luke, no doubt at the time a native of that town on the Via Egnatia, knew where to find the contacts he sought. On the Sabbath he went with his guest 'to the riverside where prayer was customarily made' (Acts 16:13).

After the Exile and the resumption of the temple worship, it seems to have been found that the synagogues of the land were by no means incompatible with the more majestic rituals of the major shrine. They had, after all, preserved the identity of Jewry. They had done more, for it was in exile in strange lands that the Jews had gathered their Scriptures together. The Psalms were collected and edited at the end of this period, and a tradition of reverence for the text of Scripture, its transmission, preservation and regular reading, was the gift of the synagogue.

Such assemblies of Jews were called 'synagogues' or 'gatherings together' by the Greeks, who thus rendered the Aramaic *kinneseth* of like meaning. (The word survives in Israel's Knesset). The buildings, which took the same name, thronged through the land. It is said that when Jerusalem fell in AD 70 there were in the city and environs some 480 synagogues, as many as in Israeli Jerusalem today.

Wherever in the Empire (and outside it as the list of expatriate Jews of Acts 2 shows) there were ten Jews together, there could be a 'synagogue', notional or material. As soon as a congregation was large enough to meet the price, a building would be erected. A conspicuous place seems to have been boldly sought, and the building had no predetermined format, based on Solomon's Temple, or anything else traditional. It could be circular or rectangular, with single or double colonnade after the prevailing Hellenistic fashions of architecture. There would be a good deal of carved ornamentation, screened commonly of any device thought idolatrous. The *menorah* or seven-branched 'candlestick' would be frequent, or the pot of manna, the 'star of David', or pomegranates.

If the surviving stones round the synagogue of Capernaum belong, as they probably do, to the first building on the site, the double-eagle sign of the Tenth Legion must have been tolerated by the Rabbis, inhibited from objections by the munificence of the gift they had received from the sympathetic centurion (Luke 7:4,5).

The synagogue was a preaching place, and the symbol of coherence. Jews, as the corpus of Scripture grew, became the 'people of a book', like the Englishmen after Elizabeth the First who gave their country the Bible. The synagogues held the Scriptures, and around its strong ethical standards, its tales of old triumph, endurance and the sense of divine destiny which arose from its whole witness, a self-conscious, proud patriotism grew. The synagogue broke the stranglehold of metropolitan Jewry on the Jewish nation as a global entity, while retaining deftly a role of leadership which was recognised by the worldwide paying of a temple tax and pilgrimage to the Holy City.

At Passover the city of Jerusalem must have been cosmopolitan indeed. Paul, who had brought the 'collection' which he hoped would signify a Christian unity between those 'scattered abroad' and the home group, and made small headway in the process, was unfortunate enough to be recognised by Ephesian Jews for the Roman citizen, Hellenistic innovator, and Christian that he was. World Jewry had already shown their hand against him (Acts 20:3), an indication that a nexus of communication existed between the synagogues, of the sort which it seems the church inherited (Acts 28:14,15). It was not only in the homeland that unrest among the Jews was beginning to create conditions for the outbreak of the dangerous and disastrous Jewish Revolt. The principates of Trajan and Hadrian knew fierce outbursts in more than one city of Jewish rebellion and civil violence.

For the spreading evangelism of the Christian church the remarkable institution of the synagogue made a mesh of witness through the whole Mediterranean world. There is some evidence of wide appeal which the pagans, especially their women, found in the austere modes of synagogue worship and the ethical values of the Jewish religion. It was a hungry world, sickened by the pagan cults which flooded into the great cities. The worship of Asian Cybele had been, for example, known in Rome long since. Isis was a later importation. In the second century before Christ the Senate had sought to deal sternly with the ecstatic rites of Dionysus. The Empire now no longer tried. Augustus' policy was two-sided. With some reluctance he allowed the east to worship Rome and the Emperor. In Italy he sought to promote the old moral values of early Rome, aided by Vergil, Horace and other poets with probably some measure of success.

It was obviously a world weary of its past and seeking a faith. Nothing, before the Christian gospel burst upon it, could compete with Judaism, and where the synagogue was strong it probably won many proselytes. And through the same synagogues, sometimes rejected out of hand, sometimes accepted (Acts 17:11), the Christian message ran like a fire. Paul, like Christ, began with the prepared ground of the synagogue, and it may be a measure of the global coherence of the Jewish expatriate communities, that the course of events so frequently followed the pattern of the homeland.

Synagogue to church

Thus it came about that, apart from providing evangelists with a first contact with the community, the institution of the synagogue prepared the path for the spread of the Christian message in many ways.

First, it enshrined, as we have seen, the Scriptures, as a sacred possession. It promoted the passionate monotheism which was the Jews' deepest conviction and a great witness to an idol-ridden world. The order of service was formal and reverent, equal to the pattern of the most strongly liturgical services of the church today. But, above all, it called for the asseveration contained in the *Shema* ('Hear . . .'). 'Hear, O Israel, the Lord our God is One'. Other words from Scripture and in formal prayer might accompany this sentence, but the great assertion itself stood magnificently out. It would be that which would stand most conspicuously in the mind of any who heard the Jewish service, and point the appeal of Judaism to thoughtful pagans. Most certainly it did prepare the way for the God of the Christians. With many pagans, the Stoics, for example, to whom Paul spoke in Athens, there was a tacit assumption that God was One (Acts 17:22-28). Judaism was emphatic.

Secondly, the synagogue prepared the way for the regular assembly of worshippers together. In all pagan cults, even the more dignified and austere, the exercise of worship was likely to be a public act in celebration of a festival or formal thanksgiving. To be sure, the exotic cults which were thronging the great cities had their regular and secret ceremonies, but not quite like the ordered assemblies of the synagogue. Consider, for example, the cult of Mithras, that stern, male religion, which withstood Christianity among Rome's legionaries. Christianity, in fact, as an act of spiritual sabotage, was to adapt and adopt from Mithraism December 25 as a festival of birth, carols, and some features of the common meal. But Mithraic devotees heard no sermon, had no pattern of spiritual instruction or exhortation, and were preoccupied with their rituals of ordeal and initiation.

Thirdly, the synagogues bequeathed the sermon to the church as a central act of worship. True, the Stoics, some of whom travelled the world with their message, and spoke in the open air with something approaching evangelical fervour, had adopted the sermon and in a way invented it outside any Jewish context. There are one or two satires of Horace, which seem to envisage an audience and heckling, that may have been moulded on the Stoic 'diatribe' — the school's word for sermon.

But the synagogue was the sermon's chief origin. The institution of preaching was promoted by Jewish tradition in the most extravagant terms. The Divine Spirit rested on the preacher and conferred on him as much merit as any act of altar sacrifice. He glorified God, quenched the thirst of men, and obeyed a command as old as Moses, who had directed that the law, the festivals and all else religious should be by word of mouth explained to the people. We read of the Rabbis preaching, in Greek or Latin, in the synagogues of Rome, as the apostles preached in Greek in the synagogues of the Dispersion. This practice, which assumed absolute liberty of teaching, was an important pathway to the evangelisation of the world. A Rabbi or distinguished stranger was known to be in town. He would be formally asked to lead in exhortation or exposition (Acts 13:14,15).

In typical fashion, the rabbinical writers, who could leave nothing undefined or unelaborated, described the good preacher. He should be of good appearance, pleasant expression, fluent, of melodious voice. He must be conciliatory and not personal. It was even perversely maintained that Moses was not permitted to bring the people into the land of promise because he had berated them as hard and rebellious. Elijah was replaced by Elisha because he had called the people to account for their breaking of the covenant, and Isaiah had been touched on the lips with a burning coal because he had boldly said that he lived among a people of unclean lips ... Such extravagances of interpretation apart, the Rabbis insisted that the preacher must know the Bible. He must carefully prepare his subject; in their word, he must 'hear himself' before he could expect others to hear him. From rabbinical literature, in fact, a considerable corpus of hermeneutical instruction could be collected, some of it for all time relevant.

Hence a revealing background for the ministry of the Lord and his apostles. The Jewish world was accustomed to the popular preacher who could adapt and apply scriptural truth to the current situation, and the Sermon on the Mount is abundant illustration of how the Lord did this, and with what acceptance – 'the common people heard him gladly . . .' Other types of preacher find place in the same rather pointless literature – the dry expositor, and the mock-modest preacher, who first refuses the honour of being called by the synagogue ruler to speak, and is reluctantly led to the lectern. The natural manner of the Lord at the Nazareth synagogue, receiving the roll, reading and sitting down to speak, is in notable contrast with such absurdities.

All rabbinical extravagance apart, however, it is obvious that the synagogue prepared the way, quite magnificently, for the Christians' preaching. Preaching was the front of the Christians' assault on the pagan world. It is a course in hermeneutics to observe how the sermons of Peter and Paul met the obvious requirements – the search for a familiar background in experience for introduction, in the Old Testament for audiences instructed in its language (witness Peter's five sermons given in briefest outline by Luke), in philosophy (Paul in Athens, singling out the Stoics as within reach), in natural theology (observe Paul seeking contact with a back-country congregation at Lystra).

The synagogue had, of course, its social uses. It was often the venue for schooling, a place of assembly for a common meal, and the Christian church in due course, when it could move from the home to more formal places of meeting, inherited such functions. The synagogue, in fact, in most Greek communities, must have looked like a church – a rostrum as its central feature and a consecrated area before it where the Scriptures were stored. Christians, especially of the more 'protestant' variety, would have felt quite at home.

Christ moved in a familiar way, in a familiar world. He came to a religious pattern and system, laid hold of it and turned it to his ends. So did his followers, and in the process there is much for us to learn – a point to which it will be appropriate for us to turn in conclusion.

CHAPTER TEN

The Pharisees

What the name means
Writing of events in 145 BC, in his *Antiquities* (13.5.9), Josephus remarks that the Pharisees, the Sadducees and the Essenes represented the religious situation in the land. In the New Testament the first two hold the stage, though the 'third force', of which the Essenes were a part, are to be seen throughout the story of the Gospels. Josephus' division is useful, and can provide sections for study and description.

The Pharisees, in unholy and unusual alliance with the Sadducees, were involved in the crime of Christ's trial and crucifixion, and that tragic mistake gave the word 'Pharisee' its evil meaning. 'Pretensions to a superior sanctity', listed by the Oxford English Dictionary as one of the marks of the sect, led to the meaning 'self-righteous hypocrite', documented in English as far back as 1589. James Russell Lowell, of Boston's Golden Age of American literature, uses it in this sense, and can provide prime illustration:

> *I du believe in Freedom's cause,*
> *Ez fur away ez Payris is,*
> *I love to see her stick her claws*
> *In them infarnal Phayrisees . . .*

Renan remarked on the manner in which Christ's words spring from the text of the New Testament with a brilliance and splendour all their own, and this is why his denunciation of the Pharisees so holds the attention, and obscures the fact that, even in the narrative of Christ's ministry, the brief period of their most lamentable choice, much is to be found in their favour. Matt. 23:13-39 is not the whole story. It is the teaching of the 'scribes', the legal experts among them, and the professional elaborators of the oral law, which the Lord's condemnation principally had in view (Mark 7:8-13). Their failure to reconcile the written and the oral law, largely a code of their own making, had made them into the blind leaders of the blind of the classic denunciation of Matt. 23. They had become impediments in the path of true religion. A pernicious gap between profession and practice was the origin of the hypocrisy which Christ described in Isaiah's words (Mark 7:6,7; Isa. 29:13). It should, however, in justice be noted that rabbinical literature itself condemns in more than one passage the hypocrisy which Christ castigated. The Talmud is as severe on the vice as Christ was.

But note that the Gospels also tell of Nicodemus (John 3), who for privacy came to Christ by night to ask when 'the kingdom' would come, and heard of another kingdom, based on Ezek. 36 and 37. He heeded the message, or why did he speak for Christ before a hostile Sanhedrin (John 7:50), and perform, along with another Sanhedrist, no doubt a fellow Pharisee, the act of notable bravery recorded in John 19:39? (See Mark 15:43; Luke 23:50-53; John 19:38). Gamaliel, a notable scholar, pleaded for tolerance (Acts 5:34-39). Other Pharisees gave friendly warning (Luke 13:31), and hospitality (Luke 7:36-38;11:37;14:1). It may be assumed that originally the sect viewed the ministry of Christ with favour, but that opposition hardened in face of the claims to a unique rôle which he made and maintained. He placed his own person in the central place, where Pharisaism placed the law, as God's revelation to man. Further, he demanded more than the law (Luke 17:10), whereas the Pharisees saw the keeping of the law as their very redemption. This self-deception was to be woven into Christian teaching on the law by Paul, himself a Pharisee of distinction, who saw, in final blinding realisation, what the law really was.

But to return to the word 'Pharisee' itself. It seems to derive from a Hebrew verb which means 'to separate'. They were, in a word, the 'separatists'. But from what? From the peril of Hellenism, with its corrosive effect on the stern, exclusive Hebrew faith? From the Gentile world, those 'lesser breeds without the law'? From the mass of the population at large who, in their ignorance and daily preoccupations, could not keep pace with the absorbing and continual demands of the Pharisaic code on the minutiae of life? Probably all of these, though some have said that the 'separatist' was one skilled to 'divide the word of truth', and separate petty wrong from equally petty right. A few have even suggested that 'Pharisee' derives from the Aramaic for 'Persian', and was a nickname for those who 'Persianized' the law, introducing the prohibitions of Zoroastrianism.

Their history

The party, at any rate, derived from the Hasidim or 'holy men' of the second century before Christ, who formed a front against Hellenism. They provided leadership in the years after 167 BC, when the mad policies of Antiochus Epiphanes tried to break the stern purity and exclusiveness which, born during the Exile in the faithful remnant of Jewry, seemed to the Syrian king's orderly mind to form a menace to his society (1 Macc. 2:42;7:13; 2 Macc. 14:6). The Hasidim were those who, according to Ezra's behest (Ezra 6:21), were determined to separate themselves from the 'filthiness of the heathen' by the careful observance of all traditional ordinances.

With the attainment of religious freedom after the success of the Maccabean war of liberation, the Pharisees found themselves thrust out of political leadership by ruling groups, ultimately to cohere into the powerful Sadducees, and such societies as the Herodians, visible in the New Testament narratives. There is no occasion here to trace the intricacies of this political rivalry. It is sufficient to show the background of the situation in Christ's time. The Pharisees, largely middle class, and numbering, says Josephus, no more than 6000, became a memorial of the movement their earlier activities had represented, and gave themselves to the elaboration of the Law they had so rightly set out to guard and strengthen.

In the New Testament they appear as the experts who took it upon themselves to pronounce upon the orthodoxy of any religious situation or event (John 1 and 9), uttering the final judgement upon it. Hence their occasional alignment against Christ with their natural opponents, the Sadducees (Matt. 16:1), and the Herodians, a society dedicated to the support and the promotion of the royal house (Matt. 22:15,16; Mark 3:6 and 12:13). They were thus of sufficient power and prestige to command hearing in the Sanhedrin. According to Josephus, the Sadducees had to recognise a wide area of popular support behind their rival sectaries, and it is striking to observe their capitulation before Gamaliel's quiet intervention.

The Pharisees seem to have opposed the great rebellion against Rome (AD 66-70), and to have largely extricated themselves from it. During, or just after, the shocking years of conflict they were permitted to establish rabbinical schools at Tiberias which successfully perpetuated Judaism. The Temple, and all it represented, was lost, and all hope of restoration vanished after the second revolt in the time of Hadrian (AD 132). Hence the final triumphs of Pharisaism in the second century, when, based on Galilee, the word became synonymous with Judaism, another page of religious history which lies outside the present theme.

The clash with the Pharisees

The movements of men, it is said, solidify into monuments and end by becoming mere memorials. So it was with Pharisaism. To preserve the noble Hebrew heritage from foreign contagion, and from the corrupting influences of Greeks and Romans, was a worthy aim. Greek thought had a seductive power, and it penetrated beneficently many alien cultures. It was destined to produce the outlook and patterns of thought which made such men as Paul, Stephen and Philip. It was to provide a language for the New Testament. But this was to happen at a certain 'fullness of time', and there was a time in history when the Greek tendency to scepticism and to questioning could have contaminated Judaism destructively.

The Pharisees may be fairly credited with blocking this path, and the fact that the common people favoured them against their rivals has a wider explanation than the fact that their rivals were predominantly the selfish collaborators with the occupying power. The Pharisaic fraternity undoubtedly must have justified to some extent a reputation for righteousness which was real. The Pharisaic achievement may, indeed, be illustrated by the one clear fact that idolatry, against which the Old Testament to its last pages wages unremitting war, is not an issue in the Gospels. The Pharisees destroyed this haunting malady of the Hebrew mind. Paul, wandering round Athens, and viewing its art, found the 'graven images', from Athene on the Acropolis to the *hermae* of each common door, a load upon his spirit.

Some law, if not Satan himself, finds 'work for idle hands to do'. Excluded from much, by rival scheming, and their own separatism, the Pharisees had time to elaborate the law. Their zeal for the Scriptures solidified into deadening rigidity. They elaborated a doctrine that, along with the written law of the Pentateuch, Moses had received an oral law, which found expression in the traditions of men. This the scribes set out to elaborate and expand, and a corpus of literature grew out of their perverse efforts which only those with time and leisure for unbroken study could understand.

Consider the revered and beneficent institution of the Sabbath. It was a healthy provision for man to set aside a seventh day for rest. So the Lord looked upon it, and it was the chief point of confrontation with the Pharisees, who had made Sabbath observance a burden unbearable. As Alfred Edersheim remarked in his century-old but still invaluable book: 'On no other subject is rabbinic teaching more painfully minute and more manifestly incongruous to its professed object.' And that object was to secure relief from labour, and make one day a delight. The same Victorian authority lists in an appendix (*The Life and Times of Jesus the Messiah* app. XVII) the prohibitions and escape clauses which occupy great tracts of rabbinical literature and which cluttered the observance of the Sabbath – matters which 'one would scarcely imagine a sane intellect would seriously entertain'. Through sixty-four folio columns in the Jerusalem Talmud, and 156 double pages of folio in the Babylon Talmud, the regulations drag on. One 'saintly' Rabbi is alleged to have spent between two and three years in the study of one of the twenty-four divisions.

One might seriously discuss whether an ass might or might not be led on to the road with a covering on, unless the said covering had been put in place before the Sabbath dawned. One could, on the other hand, lead the animal about in one's own courtyard. Or, if the road was narrow, could one convert an alley into one's own house by placing a beam from door to door? Before such nonsense one Rabbi is said ecstatically to have declared that such Sabbath rules were like mountains suspended by a hair. No trace of concern for the spiritual, or the divine, purpose of the Sabbath is to be discerned amid such massive folly.

It is idle to pursue such a subject further, but note that the Sabbath was only a section of the total corpus of such literature upon which the scribes expended their perverse ingenuity. A mythology grew alongside – the Sabbath river which did not flow on the seventh day, the ass which would not eat oats which had not been tithed . . .

It became impossible to keep the Sabbath, even for the ingenious inventors of such regulations. That is why there exists, alongside the regulations, an equally voluminous corpus of escape clauses designed to make a legal exit from the labyrinth for those lost in it. For example, it was illegal to eat an egg laid on the Sabbath. But if one stated before the Sabbath that the hen likely to commit such an abomination was destined for the table, the egg might then be legitimately eaten, because it was merely an object which had dropped from an already doomed bird.

Similarly with grace over meat. Eating good food and thanking God for such a gift was, and is, a simple enough process. The

Pharisees fell into interminable discussion whether one grace could cover all items at table, or whether each demanded a special ritual of gratitude. It was settled, after much solemn debate, that the blessing pronounced over the principal item covered all else – but not what may be called dessert. There were elaborate discussions over the blessing pronounced on fruit. The caper, for example, caused deep controversy over whether fruit, leaves and blossom could be comprehended in one act of grace. The schools of Shammai and Hillel divided on the issue. Such weighty questions exercised the minds of Pharisees and scribes, and such matters could fill volumes and preoccupy debate for endless hours. One can be certain that the Jews, who had sworn not to eat until they had killed Paul, did not starve. Any number of verbal tricks could free them for continued sustenance (Acts 23:12,13).

It was the spiritual and psychological damage which such day and nightlong preoccupations did to those entertaining such thought which was the most serious aspect of Pharisaism. When life is made unbearable under the bondage of such demanding legalism, and it becomes necessary to secure casuistical relief, serious damage is done to the personality. At every step, in taking a meal, in performing the carefully regulated ablutions before a meal, in the home, outside the home, the truly dedicated Pharisee was overwhelmed with paralysing formulae of conduct. It was impossible for a healthy spiritual life to exist under such a burden.

Hence the encouragement of open hypocrisy. The rabbis Gidal and Jochanan, for example, rebuked for their habit of sitting in the women's bathing-place, claimed that they were of the lineage of Joseph, over whom sin had no power – forgetting Joseph's flight from temptation. It is easy to imagine how such pernicious self-deception poisoned the springs of true morality. Such a habit of mind led to the hardness of heart which Christ could view only as a 'sin against the Holy Spirit'. Such minds could so damage spiritual understanding, so obscure any saving apprehension of God, that Christ could pronounce such personalities as doomed beyond redemption, already lost in condemnation.

As to what might have been regarded as the prime function of those who claimed spiritual leadership and holiness, how could such an office be fulfilled, if obedience were made so hopeless, except for those who knew every detail of the law, and also the escape clauses which made it possible to live? Such 'experts' could hardly be other than inveterate deceivers of the world at large, and ultimately, such is the judgement which lies upon such sin, of the offenders themselves. He who makes a guest of sin soon ceases to be the host.

Hence the justification of the great denunciation of 'scribes, Pharisees and hypocrites'.

Hence, too, the utter failure of the Pharisees, as a body, to provide spiritual leadership, which was their proper opportunity and office. They became 'blind leaders of the blind', 'false shepherds who care not for the sheep', 'usurpers of the vineyard' ... Many of the parables of Easter week laid bare these faults, and deepened the determination of their hardened members to accept a painful alliance with the Sadducees, and so be rid of One who so ruthlessly exposed their faults. Such was the tragedy of the sect. They had exalted righteousness and won wide regard. And then they had made righteousness into a load too heavy to bear, and so deprived their people of what was their right to have. It was a justification of the Lord's stern judgement upon their abandoned state of mind that they next turned to despising the people at large – 'an accursed breed that knows not the law' (John 7:47-49).

Nothing more strikingly illustrates the splendid sanity of Jesus than his complete freedom from such bondage. Paul and Peter found the attitudes of Judaism difficult to dispel. Both apostles spent years of striving and mental battle before winning emancipation from the overwhelming power of the religion of their day, of which the Pharisees were the leaders and exemplars. Jesus seems to have found such emancipation as natural to him as the air he breathed. With exact and unerring insight he accepted all that was good, or potentially good, in the attitudes and teaching of the religious leaders of the day. With a clarity as incisive he touched on every point where the true law of Jewry was misinterpreted or distorted, and, in a manner not always adequately realised by those outside the power of that day's pretensions, laid bare in a word or phrase all deceit, all inadequacy. He accepted the law, and took it deeper than its mere letter. He showed in a word or a phrase how deep the roots of righteousness and unrighteousness lay. His powerful mind, bypassing the literal and materialistic beloved of the Pharisees, disengaged the basic principles and the spiritual realities. The sheer power of intellect, the splendid sanity and penetration of understanding in the man from the carpenter's bench in Nazareth is forceful argument for his deity. He had no master, no formative school, behind him. He had absorbed all that was good from every good teacher in Israel. As unerringly he rejected, as only perfect goodness could, all that was evil. He could face the most subtle minds of those who sought to discredit him, fall into their forms of argument at will, or as promptly discard them, and single-handed leave Jewry's best trained minds without an argument. To apprehend within its historical context this agility of intellect, is to be convinced that here was a Person who justified in every encounter the claim he made to have come 'from above'.

CHAPTER ELEVEN

Sadducees and Essenes

What the name means?

As with the word 'Pharisee', 'Sadducee' stands in some semantic doubt. According to a Jewish legend, traceable no further back than the seventh century of our era, the word derives from one Tsadok (or Zadok) who deprecated serving God for reward. Others, with an eye to the fact that the Sadducees seem to have had high prominence in the priesthood, have derived their name from Solomon's high priest Zadok. Josephus seems to know nothing of this, and linguists find difficulties in the vowel. Names are usually given to groups or orders by their opponents. Witness the word 'Christian', or 'Methodist'. On the assumption, then, that the *Hasidim* or 'pious ones' were dubbed 'Pharisees' by public usage, it could be that those who did not follow the preoccupations of the 'pious ones' might retort that they were satisfied to be called the 'righteous ones' (*Tsaddiqim*), and have the term popularly accepted. Hence 'Sadducees', the linguistic difficulty, which persists, being accountable to popular usage – and, according to Edersheim (*The Life and Times of Jesus the Messiah*, 1. 324), promoted by a subtle witticism which need not detain us. Nor need another radical explanation, which derives the word from Greek.

The first use of the name goes back to Josephus' account of the Maccabean war of liberation, and the passage already quoted in reference to the Pharisees, but the tangled history of the group's struggle for power in the early Sanhedrin is not relevant to the present purpose, which concerns the position of the Saducean priesthood in the time of Christ's ministry. In those events they played a vital part. There were Pharisees on the Sanhedrin and Pharisees among the priests, but it does appear from the Gospels that, although not all-powerful, and dependent to a considerable extent on the compliance of the Pharisees, the Saducees dominated the hierarchy. They were predominantly from aristocratic and wealthy families.

Difference from Pharisees

It is wrong to see the Saducees as the direct opposition to the Pharisees on such themes as Hellenisation, the Temple clergy as distinct from the synagogue-based laity, the political as against the religious wing of the hierarchy. The two groups argued and manifested distinct doctrinal differences, of which more below, but it is difficult, along a wide front, to establish a sharp distinction and opposition. The union of Pharisees and Saducees in final opposition to Christ could easily have had other facets than this momentous partnership in crime.

There were sharp doctrinal difficulties. The Saducees, while not averse to some of the Pharisaic traditions, were not prepared, and rightly so, to admit that the oral law went back to Moses. Their concern in this matter may have been to keep in their own priestly hands the prerogative of interpreting Moses. Their stand, however, forced them into formulating their own corpus of rules and regulations, hardly to be separated in principle from the corpus of Pharisaic regulations. But to insist on the priority of the written law of Moses was undoubtedly in conformity with the Saducees' concern for the temple ritual and its purity.

Another area of difference was that of predestination and free will, the ancient arena of fruitless contention and controversy, into which the over-logical of all time have been forced when attempting to codify the dealings of God with man. The Pharisees, according to Josephus, sought a synthesis, the Essenes attributed all to 'Fate', adopting the Greek concept embodied in that word. The rival Saducees, on the other hand, attributed everything to free will.

The Saducees, further, denied the resurrection of the dead or anything in the nature of reward or punishment after death, a matter of difference with the Pharisees of which Paul took full advantage on the occasion of his arraignment before the Sanhedrin (Acts 23:6-10). This doctrinal stance contributed richly to the Saducees' worldly attitude. If this life is all, human nature concludes that present advantage and advancement is a logical enough conclusion. Along with such a belief went rejection of the Messianic hope and a spiritual world. The latter may have been an over-reaction to the elaborate systems of 'angelology' and hierarchies of heavenly beings which proliferated in the period between the Testaments, and proved, as Paul found at Colossae in the Lycus Valley, a problem even for the Christian church. There may be seen a certain logic in the claim of the Sadducees to be the conservative guardians of the pure code of Moses, which their rivals had elaborated and expanded beyond all recognition.

The Sadducees and Christ

It was natural enough that the Pharisees should be the first to clash with Christ. He moved among the masses from which the more aristocratic Sadducees were somewhat removed. Sadducees appeared by Jordan when the Pharisees were engaged on the investigation of the desert preacher, and earned his fierce denunciation (Matt. 3; John 1). They appear with the events of Matthew 16 (1,6,11,12), and even in this context earn no mention in the parallel passage of Mark. Jesus coupled the 'leaven' of both sects only in the sense that he regarded both as equally pernicious in doctrine. At the end of Jesus' ministry in Jerusalem, the Sadducees appeared among his questioners where they met prompt defeat on Mosaic grounds – appropriately enough (Matt. 22:23-33; Mark 12:18-27; Luke 20:27-38; compare Exod. 3:6).

It became clear with the cleansing of the Temple of what was undoubtedly Sadducean commerce, that Christ was a danger to their order. On this occasion he baffled them, for the account in John 2 in no way suggests violence. He no doubt stood with a bunch of discarded cattle halters in his hand, and, by the mere force and power of his prestige, promoted uneasiness, fumbling, and the development of a stampede among the beasts. He needed no personal action to 'overturn the tables of the money changers'. The stampede of animals would account for that, without violence on the agent's part. It is quite significant that the authorities had no specific charge to level against him. It follows that he had done nothing indictable (John 2:14-18). The conspiracy with the Pharisees developed forthwith (John 11:57). Collaboration followed (Mark 14:53-15:5).

The Sadducees' opposition to the apostles also followed (Acts 4:1-22;5:17-42). With the fall of Jerusalem and the end of the Temple, the Sadducees disappear from history. They had formed, over the whole period of the Lord's ministry, the collaborators with Rome, and it suited those realists in their imperial policy to foster and promote the interests and standing of the Sadducees. It was when the

Lord began to take shape in their wary eyes as a possible disturber of their delicate relationship with Rome that Caiaphas uttered his cynical opinion that such a peril should be removed, even at the risk of some injustice (John 11:49,50).

The Herodians, mentioned three times in the story of Easter Week (Matt. 22:16; Mark 3:6 and 12:13), were probably a sub-group of the Sadducees. They were such a society as any modern country can show, committed to the promotion of some special common interest, or pledging loyalty to one political figure. Their attachment was to the royal house. Augustus enjoyed the support of a similar group in Rome. Perhaps the Herodians were an activist group among the Sadducees, who saw the political stability of the royal house and its policies as the ground of their own safety and stability in a dangerously exclusive society, and therefore combined to support it.

The Essenes

The third group mentioned by Josephus make no visible appearance in the New Testament but are discernible in the narrative. They were desert dwellers, and from them and allied groups the first church drew many converts. They were the 'third force' in the land, faithful folk who saw neither in the Pharisees nor in the Sadducees the true custodians of the Law or the posterity of Moses.

The fact that there were protest movements in Jewish religion has always been known, and Isaiah's 'make straight in the desert a pathway for your God' was a strong command in the minds of some who reacted against city corruption and material sin. The Essenes, described by Pliny, the Roman writer who lost his life in the eruption of Vesuvius, were, as the discovery of Qumran and the Dead Sea Scrolls demonstrates, only one of several such communities in the Jordan Valley. They varied in rules and outlook but their theme was the same, withdrawal, asceticism and devotion to the Bible. The modern kibbutz movement in some ways follows them.

In speaking of the Dead Sea, Pliny writes:

> On its west side, just far enough to avoid its baneful influences, live the Essenes. They form a solitary community and they inspire our admiration more than any other community in the whole world. They live without women, for they have renounced all sex life; they live without money, and without any company save that of the palm-trees. From day to day their numbers are maintained by the stream of people who seek them out and join them from far and wide. These people are driven to adopt the Essenes' way of life through weariness of ordinary life and by reason of a change of fortune. Thus, through thousands of

generations – incredible to relate – this community in which no one is ever born continues without dying; other people's weariness of life is the secret of their abiding fertility. Below their headquarters was the town of Engedi, whose fertility and palm-groves formerly made it second only to Jerusalem; but now, like Jerusalem itself, it lies in a heap of ashes. Next comes Masada, a fortress on a rock, itself also not far from the Dead Sea. And there is the frontier of Judea.

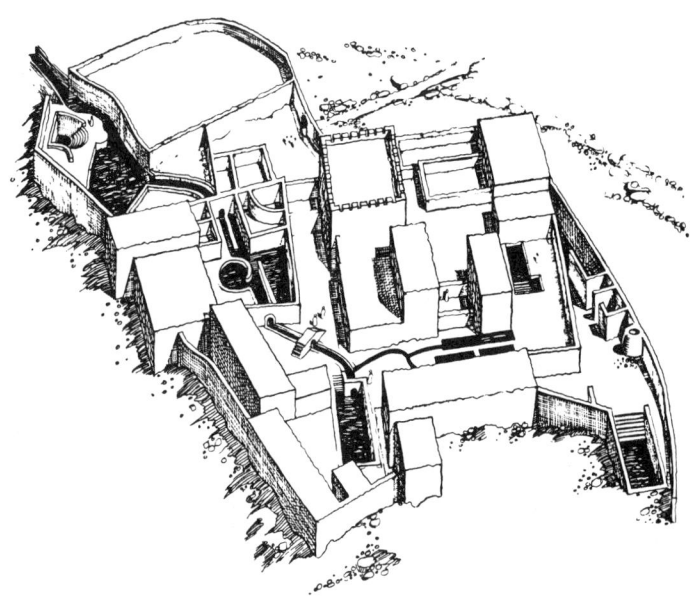

The monastery at Qumran

It is typical of a too common kind of Victorian scepticism that Hastings' *Dictionary of the Bible*, in an article of over eighty-five years ago, dismissed Pliny's account of an ascetic community by the Dead Sea as mistaken. With the library from the caves to point the way, the archaeologists turned to a ruin at Qumran, and found it to be just such a place as Pliny described, a sort of monastery but without celibacy, as skeletal remains of both men and women reveal, the home of a dedicated fellowship given to discipline, the preservation of the Scriptures, and to holy living. The community was established about 135 BC. It continued for almost exactly two hundred years. In AD 66 came the mad revolt of the Jews against the Romans, over three years of grim and awful warfare, the destruction of Jerusalem, and the systematic ransacking of Palestine for all remnants of Jewish opposition. To the Romans, in the days of the Great Revolt, such folk were partisans, and Vespasian's troops overran and destroyed the buildings. The inhabitants, no doubt, escaped, for they had time to hide their books in the caves. 'This treasure we have in earthen vessels', said Paul, and he was alluding to a custom observed at Qumran. The books were concealed in great jars of earthenware.

Here then is a vivid if not quite accurate Roman picture of a Jewish community remote from the urban preoccupations and practices of the hierarchy of the Sadducees, and the twin schools of Pharisaism. It was one of many such groups, with associates throughout the land, by no means all of them remote and separated from the tasks of industry and daily living. And it is a fact implicit in the Gospels that Christ sought his first followers and disciples among the poor of the land, outside organised religion. Hence, the meaning of the Dead Sea Scrolls for Christians of today. It may be summed up in three exhortations. Let them seek simplicity in their faith, and avoid the perils of social compromise. Let them find unity in a common devotion to their God. Let them be prepared to see the benison of heaven rest rather on the devoted than the proud, on the humble rather than the great.

But such has ever been the theme and purport of the New Testament, and if Qumran is, as one writer put it, to rank with Bethlehem and Nazareth as 'a cradle of Christianity', it is in this sense that the tendentious words could be true. John translated passive protest and retreat into action, revival and return, if Toynbee's formula may be applied. And since John's converts provided the first Christian disciples and prepared the land for the impact of Christ, Qumran, if John was influenced by the group, may claim a preparatory part.

It is significant enough that John's great religious revival was centred in the Jordan's wilderness where the river joins the Dead Sea. Qumran was a few miles only away, Engedi no more than twenty-five miles along the coast. And Isaiah is quoted in the Gospels more than any other prophet. Thanks to John he was well known in Israel. And how curious it is that the prize possession of the red-robed community at Qumran is a beautiful roll of Isaiah, now housed in the indestructible inner sanctum of Jerusalem's Shrine of the Book.

When the little band at Qumran fled before the cohorts who were mopping up the pockets of resistance in the lower Jordan, Christianity was already established in major centres from Alexandria to Antioch and Rome. The land was dying, but the scattered sparks of a new faith were spreading the fire through the Empire.

It was perhaps in AD 68 in the midst of the Great Revolt that the patrols, who were clearing the Jordan valley, found and burnt Qumran. That was the last year of Nero's principate. Four years earlier, Nero had made the Christians of Rome – 'a vast number', according to Tacitus, the historian – the scapegoats for Rome's great fire. Almost twenty years earlier, if the Nazareth Decree is rightly judged a rescript of Claudius, Nero's imperial predecessor had heard the Pharisees' explanation of the empty tomb. Seven years earlier still, the same Claudius had chided the Jews of Alexandria for turbulence, and appears to make a reference to Christian missionaries. Jerusalem and its church were gone. The Christians fled to Pella in time. The religious communities of the Essenes and their group disappeared. There is evidence in the great fortress of Masada, near the southern end of the Dead Sea, that some from Qumran joined the garrison in the three years' fruitless resistance which ended the Roman subjugation. Some Qumran-like literature has been found there.

Such then was the religious situation in the land when Christ came, and his disciples founded the church. The crime of his death lay with the hierarchy. Whether the desert communities knew of him is not known, but they must have known John, and John's net was wide. He influenced fisher-folk from Galilee at the other end of the Valley. He influenced the guerrillas, already appearing in the land, or how else would a 'Zealot' appear in the list of the apostles? Jews, whose lives were changed, and who owed an allegiance to John, were found at Ephesus more than twenty years later (Acts 19:1-7). The desert communities must, therefore, perhaps knowing little of it, have played a preparatory part.

Chapter Twelve

Lessons for Today

Then and now

In conclusion, we should ask where this study has led us, and what wisdom may be derived from the knowledge gained. It is almost thirty years since the Cambridge historian, Professor Herbert Butterfield, published his remarkable book, *Christianity and History*. A wise paragraph in his last chapter could well afford us a useful conclusion. Butterfield pointed out that, after a period of fifteen centuries, it may be safely said today that it no longer pays to be a Christian. No one professes the Faith today because of some authoritarian compulsion, to obtain some favour or preferment, public office, status or advantage. Integrity, and true faith which guarantees it, may still be valued in decent society, but no man comes to Christ today in order to demonstrate some worth or orthodoxy which may please neighbours or superiors, multiply clients or gain customers, or provide that smoother path or that comfort in society which a safe conformity too often in history has guaranteed.

'This fact', wrote Butterfield, 'makes the present day the most important and the most exhilarating period in the history of Christianity for fifteen hundred years; and the removal of so many kinds of inducement and compulsion makes nonsense of any argument based on the decline in the numbers of professing Christians in the twentieth century. We are back for the first time in something like the earliest centuries of Christianity, and those early centuries afford some relevant clues to the kind of attitude to adopt.'

In other words, we are back for the first time to where the church began, facing an indifferent, increasingly bewildered and often hostile society. We are back to the days where, sometimes even under professedly tolerant regimes, too often under tyrannies as old as time, the temptation is as pressing as the Nicolaitans found it, to modify an uncompromising stance, to placate 'the world', and bridge a painful gap by damaging surrender. The 'Remnant' of the Old Testament is in confrontation with evil again; the honoured Few are on the stage of time. And how often has history seen 'the Few' make impact on their century out of all proportion to their numbers!

The cities

One sphere in which this century is more like the first than any of the rest which lie between, is its city-ridden character. Great conurbations like Rome, Athens, Corinth, Alexandria, tended to dominate politics and determine the atmosphere of the time.

Paul of all people knew this, and it is interesting, and enormously instructive, to see his pattern of evangelism. He sought to plant his colonies of Christians in key cities – Antioch in Pisidia, the bastion of Roman power in central Asia Minor; Ephesus, the religious centre of the province of Asia and the ruling proconsul's seat; Thessalonica, at the eastern terminus of the Egnatian Way; Athens, the great centre of the world's learning; Corinth, nodal point of Mediterranean trade – not to mention Rome itself, as grim and hostile and dangerous a place as Juvenal, the embittered satirist, found it forty years later. Paul even had in mind Spain, the third peninsula (Rom. 15:24). He was clearly offering the great system the cement it increasingly sought in the Caesar-cult.

Paul, of course, expected his churches to penetrate the hinterland. Observe how Ephesus did precisely this. At the end of one of those radiating valleys, which form the geographical shape of Asia Minor's blunt western end, Ephesus formed a diffusion point for the trade-routes which climbed them. The 'seven churches' of Revelation 2 and 3, together with Hierapolis and Colossae, all lay at the head of such valley roads, three of them in the Lycus Valley alone. All were Ephesian in their origin and foundation. The church at Ephesus had functioned well.

The measure of some failure of the church at large so to spread lies in the very word 'pagan'. *Pagani* were simply people who lived in a *pagus* or village, country folk, who became 'pagans' in another sense, because so few of them had heard the city-based gospel of Christ. But Paul saw clearly enough that if the Empire, of which he was, rarely for a Jew, an accredited citizen, was to be won for Christ, it must be a process initiated and forwarded by the great urban congregations. The vision is not dated. Christianise the great cities, and one is more than halfway towards the evangelism of the whole world. Lose the cities, and some today, from Calcutta to New York and London, seem poised upon some evasive brink, lose them to violence, degradation and corruption, and the country is also lost. Gain them, cleanse their hearts, make them fit to live in, and much on a vast front is won. The cities are a missionary field of the first order today, their withering hearts and their exploding suburbs. They must be invaded, their dead hearts evangelised in the week, if not the week-ends. They matter much.

The cities of the first century, as we have seen in passing, had all the problems which afflict great agglomerations of men still. Juvenal wrote just after John, the last apostle, had died, and his third satire, quoted in the last chapter, describes Rome, swarming with foreigners, sometimes too quick-witted for Romans to match them in the race for material gain. The city, Juvenal storms, was noisy, mean, crowded hideously, and the nesting-ground of a clutter of eastern cults, dangerous to live in, dens of the arrogant rich and a degraded proletariat.

The city proletariat – and Ephesus was a prime example – was the first difficulty the church had to face. Ruffians from the market-place (Acts 17:5) drove him from Thessalonica. A working-men's demonstration ended his work in Ephesus. In Rome, Nero found ready scapegoats when he sought to shift the blame for the fire of Rome in July AD 64 on to other heads, and fuel for his firing in the displeasure which the compliant and conforming majority feel for the dissident and non-conforming few. The Christians were disliked. The spectacle of moral earnestness, such is human nature, offends the morally inert, and the sight of disciplined living rebukes and angers self-indulgence (1 Pet. 4:4). The vested interests of vice fear virtue, and corruption is uneasy in the presence of a sterner and challenging uprightness. So, in varied fashion, had Christians stirred the emotional hostility of the ancient crowd. Nero canalised the crowd's passion, gave it self-expression, and supplied a cover of reason for baseness, and a cloak of social righteousness for unreasoning hatred. He so ravaged the church that the brutal mob itself, Tacitus tells us, began to show revulsion.

Social ostracism, therefore, in the early history of the church preceded official persecution. The Christian was at odds with society before he fell out with the State. It is possible from the New Testament to shed some light on the cruel dilemma in which he was placed, and to unearth evidence of an inner conflict which all but shattered the church. The study of the situation throws light on the principles of persecution and directs attention to some laws of Christian sociology which are by way of finding new importance in the growing paganism of the day.

The same unpopularity is to be seen in Bithynia in the text of two letters which Pliny wrote to Trajan from that province in AD 111, two priceless documents of the early church. The whole province was in the grip of a Christian revival, though who were the missionaries, who brought the message there, is quite unknown. But the letters show how a reluctant and humane governor was forced to persecute by the clamour of a cruel mob.

It is easy, from the letters, to reconstruct the situation. Pliny had received the complaints of the temple priests, and of the guild of the butchers, whose sales of 'sacrificial meat' were falling off, and of all the small community which derived profit from the functioning of pagan ritual. The Christians were tampering with the established processes of life, challenging, rebuking. As in Rome, as in Ephesus (Acts 19), the injured forces of paganism struck back with some success. The weak and the fearful fell away. The faithful and the brave died, or suffered exile. The sales of the 'idol meat' increased and the legalistic governor saw his province sink to rest. And in his letter he left a record of one of the precise moments when the social ostracism of the Christian church turned into State persecution.

How true are the words the cynical Machiavelli wrote: 'There is nothing more difficult to take in hand, more perilous to conduct ... than a new order of things, because the innovator has for enemies all those who have done well under the old conditions, and lukewarm defenders in those who do well under the new.'

To be sure, the 'innovators' who brought Christianity to the cities of the Mediterranean world, were no lukewarm defenders of their faith, but as the urban pressures grew in the great cities, there were those who sought, in agony of mind, a compromise, and we shall turn to them presently. But one cannot find a city of Paul, where the first preaching of the gospel did not provoke popular hostility. And there are today, in this vastly organised world of cities, many places where the faith is persecuted, suppressed, outlawed. It survived only by an uncompromising and perilous stand. The church, in spite of weak, mistaken and, indeed, disloyal pleas, must not try to adapt itself to the twentieth century any more than it found it could adapt itself in doctrine to the first. It is the century, if man is to live, that must adapt itself to the church. Paul puts it well (Rom. 12:1,2):

'Please, brothers, in the name of God's mercies towards us, stop trying to conform to the society around you . . .'

The Nicolaitans

There were some in the church who sought such adaptation. The early church was in mortal danger from them. It had, remember, no New Testament, no authorative written corpus of doctrine. Only the utterly uncompromising stand of the apostles, to be read throughout their epistles, brought the church through to its establishment, survival and strength. Had that first generation faltered all would have been lost. That is why the New Testament is so contemporary a document.

The early church, of which Corinth was a prime example, was ravaged by division, plagued by Judaism and other deviant doctrine, denial even of the resurrection, faulty morality and anything which can be discovered of damaging licence today. Paul's constant endeavour, as the letters to Corinth and Colossae show, was to purify and lift its feeble life. Paul was backed by Peter in this noble endeavour (2 Pet. 3:15,16). A dangerous group, active and vocal in the Christian community, had received mistakenly Paul's doctrine of freedom as a liberal philosophy, which demanded no stern separation from paganism. Paul's teaching had been distorted by the 'ill-informed and unbalanced people', of Peter's words referred to above, and were, as Peter's second letter, and Jude's related one make clear, cohering into a sect, called by the two apostles 'followers of Balaam', and later by John (Rev. 2 and 3) 'Nicolaitans', a word of unknown origin.

These seem to have been those whose trail begins in Corinth, people who found it difficult to separate themselves from a close-knit pagan society, to lose, perhaps, in so doing, their livelihood, and suffer ostracism. No balanced person enjoys being at odds with society, and in Corinth and elsewhere, the problem of membership of the trade guilds was real and agonising. Christians were sorely tempted to organise some code of compromise, as, especially under authoritarian regimes, they are tempted to do today. The problem caused tension and difficulty in the Christian community itself, as chapters 8 to 10 of the first letter to Corinth show. The last verse of Chapter 8 was the noble solution Paul suggested for such dangerous differences, and it applies, with other circumstances to give it relevance, to the church today. 'He taught us', wrote Judge Hughes of Rugby's Dr. Arnold, 'that in this world none can tell which of his actions is indifferent and which is not . . . we can lead astray a brother for whom Christ died.' Such was the core of Paul's masterly approach to Corinth, and it is relevant still. But a look must be taken at the position which developed in the church at large, as other apostles saw it.

The correlated epistles of Jude and Peter's second letter are the documents. It is clear that the problem of the Christian's place in pagan society was not yet solved, and that the deep anxieties of the last years of the founders of the church were justified. Their concern is written large in the strong language used by both Jude and Peter, and later still by John, last alive of all the Lord's men. The apostles were in no mood to leave the field they had so lovingly tended, and for which they had shed tears and blood, to the laxities of a dissident group prepared to banish from the church's life those very elements which had set it over against the world, different, stern in morals, and therefore challenging. 'Give me a place to stand', said Archimedes speaking of levers, 'and I will move the world'. So with the Christian faith. Mingled with the pagan horde, like the disciples lost in the crowd around the place of crucifixion, Christians lose leverage, and nothing vital can be done. Stand apart and a leverage results.

This is what makes Peter's, Jude's and John's epistles so very applicable today. Paul's vision of the Empire for Christ had faded, through no fault of Paul, but of the Empire. The supreme disservice to history, which the Romans had served well, was the folly of persecution. A Christian Empire, active in evangelism, might have spared the world the Middle Ages. The surviving apostles saw this with utter clarity. Hence the fierce denunciation of those who sought, by this and that form of compromise and adaptation, to sap the power of the church and its gospel to convert.

These people, mentioned by Jude and Peter, 'self-willed rebels like Korah, rainless clouds, fruitless trees, noisy surf, wandering stars, a menace to the fellowship of the Lord's Table', had 'taken the road of Cain, and perpetrated the old error of Balaam'. What does all this battery of metaphor suggest? Profession without reality, preaching without profit, pride and self-assertion, at least. And more – Cain was the symbol of carnality in worship. His graceful altar, flower-decked, was the emblem of the easy path, of religion stripped of sternness and austerity. Balaam, in the imagery of the passage, stands for the breakdown of 'separation', the effacement of those differences which mark and set apart the people of God, and the mingling of sacred and profane.

It is interesting to look a little more closely at this recurring figure of Balaam, sire of all money-seeking prelates. It appears that the sum of his advice to his employer was that Israel's strength could be sapped by the Moabite women. The stern standards of Israel's God demanded absolute separation from surrounding paganism. John saw such seducers at their damaging work again, luring Christians, newly escaped from the pervading evils of pagan society, to acts of compromise which could only take the power and purity of the church away and destroy its ability to convert.

John had some fierce words to say to a woman of Thyatira, the ancient trading town from which Paul's hostess in Philippi had come on business. Inscriptions from Thyatira mention more trade guilds – wool-workers, linen-workers, leather-workers, dyers, tanners, bakers, bronzesmiths – than are found in any other place. It must have been an extremely difficult place for Christian tradesmen, who felt called, in conscience, to abstain from the pagan-tinted proceedings of their appropriate guilds. They must have known the cutting edge of that hideous situation which John envisages in Chapter 13 of Revelation, where a universal dictator denies buying and selling to all who have not 'the mark of the beast' on hand and head – a passage frightening to read in a world of multiplying computer banks, numbered citizens, 'closed shops', and organised ostracism.

John in his severe little letter calls the woman of Thyatira, who seems to have been the leader in some programme of compromise, by the well-remembered and loathed name of Jezebel, the princess of Tyre who married Ahab, as part of a profitable trade alliance between the northern kingdom and the Phoenicians. It was a worldly-wise arrangement. Israel gained wealth. Ahab had an ivory palace, fragments of whose panelling are found upon the site, but Israel lost its chastity, its standards and its God. When Elijah brought the people back to God, if indeed that revival was something deeper than cheers on Carmel, he brought much commercial disaster on the land. But he saved its soul. In Thyatira Jezebel would be a potent symbol of the congregation's own dilemma, because there is evidence enough that the early Christian groups knew the Greek Old Testament.

It seems clear enough that the clever Thyatiran woman was one of the so-called Nicolaitans, and for this no doubt powerful group the last of the apostles had nothing but utter condemnation. They offered relief in what they considered reasoned compromise to anxious and beleaguered men and women. John saw that, in spite of the rigours of abstinence, and the popular contempt and official persecution it provoked, no relaxing of standards was possible. The way of liberalism, as so often in all history is the case, was the way of ruin.

Such is the indictment of Nicolaitanism. It suggests a deep-seated disagreement within the church itself, which affected and determined the relation of the new religion to the existing forms and character of city society. The real issue was this – should the church accept society or declare war against it? Should Christianity adapt itself to the existing forms of the world at large, or force the world to conform to its principles? It is easy to overlook the vast human problems involved. 'We are struck,' Ramsay says, 'with admiration at the unerring insight with which the Apostles gauged every question that presented itself in the complicated life of the period, and the quick, sure decision with which they seized and insisted on the essential, and neglected the accidental and secondary aspects of the case.' For a Christian of the middle class, trained by a rather elaborate education to take a somewhat artificial view of life, and to reconcile its contradictions by subtle devices. of philosophy, tenacious in a class-conscious society of caste and position, Nicolaitanism must have appeared a mental haven after storm.

Was John too harsh? Sir William Ramsay answers the question well. 'The historian,' he writes, 'must regard the Nicolaitans with intense interest, and must deeply regret that we know so little about them, and that only from their enemies. And yet at the same time he must feel that nothing could have saved the infant church from melting away into one of those vague and ineffective schools of philosophic ethics except the stern and strict rule laid down by John. An easy-going Christianity could never have survived; it could not have conquered and trained the world; only the most convinced, resolute, adherence to the most uncompromising interpretation of its own principles could have given the Christians the courage and self-reliance that were needed. For them to hesitate or to doubt was to be lost.'

The cost was heavy – in loss, in physical and mental suffering. In Nero's Rome, unpopularity begat persecution. Ephesus revealed a reaction as savage. In Bithynia, State repression followed the hostile protest of resentful paganism. In the early records of the church we see the first attempts of Christians to live at peace with paganism; we can read the warnings of Paul, and see how, in disregard of those warnings, a group emerged who abused his noble doctrine of liberty and mingled Christ determinedly with Belial. As the New Testament closes the long years of State persecution are about to open. They were to cleanse and purify the church. But the church could never have survived the impact of those years had there not been in her midst a body of men and women who literally 'counted all things but loss for Christ'. We bow the head before those who bore all the human heart finds it most difficult to bear, to preserve the faith unsullied, unadulterated, undamaged, and intact.

In conclusion hear again Professor Butterfield's significant words: 'We are back for the first time in the earliest centuries of Christianity, and those centuries afford some relevant clues to the kind of attitude to adopt.' The old situation could arise again.

Subject Index

Acropolis 91, (illus. 83)
Acts of the Apostles 39–40
Alexander 24, 40, 50, 75–76
Alexandria 77
Antioch in Pisidia 120
Antiochus Epiphanes 105
Antiquities 103
Antonius Felix 69–70
Apollos 11
appeal 72–73
Aquila 11
Aratus of Soli 92
Areopagus 81–82, 93
Armageddon 24
Athene Promachus 82, 91, 106
Athenians 81–86
Athens 81, 120
atomic theory 86
Attalus III 50
Augustus, Emperor 9, 11, 13, 14, 15–16, 18, 20–21, 27, 28, 29, 48, 51, 55
Baalam 124–125
Babylonian exile 98
Bethlehem 19–22
Britain 14
Butterfield, Professor Herbert 119, 127
Caesar, Julius 51
Caesarea 58
Caiaphas 114
Capernaum 26
Carmel 24, 25
carpentry 23
Carthage 49–50
census 27, 28, 29

centers of civilization (map) 41
centurions 26
ceremonies, Greek 78–79
Christian Church 99–102, 123
Christianity 121–123
Christians 95–96
Cicero 52–53, 87
Cimbri 11
cities 17–26, 39–46, 120
citizenship 71
civil war 50–51
Claudius Lysias 69–70
Cleanthes 88–89, 92
Cleopatra 51
climate 12
Codex Bezae 40
coins 66
Colosseum 43
commerce 11
communications 55–57
Coponius 63–64
Corinth 42, 93–94, 120
crowds 37
crucifixion 36–37, 69
Cunctator, Fabius 49
currency 66–67
Cyrene 12
Danube River 14
Dead Sea Scrolls 22, 114, 116
death rate 26
decadence 83–84
Decapolis 78
Democritus 86
Demosthenes 83–84
deserts 12–13
Dionysius 82, 93–94

Drusus 14, 21
dynasts 50–54
Egypt 13
Elijah 101
Elizabeth 19
Emperor 48
Empire, Greek 75
Empire, Greek (map) 76
Engedi 115
Ephesus 25, 40–41, 120
Epicureanism 86–94
Epicurus 87–88, 90
Epimenides 91–92
Esdraelon plain 24, 25
Essenes 103, 112, 114–117
Etruscans 49
evangelism 120
famine 26
farms 35
Fertile Crescent 12–13, 18
Galilee 35
Gallio 42
Gamaliel 20, 27, 104
Gaul 14
Gauls 49–50
Golden Age 81–84
Golden Milestone, The 57
Gospels 32–33
government, Roman 40–45, 63–73
Great Rebellion, The 44, 105, 116–117
Greece 50
Greek colonies 75–77
Greek language 77
Greeks 75–94
Hadrian 22, 26, 90
Hannibal 49
Hasidim 105, 111
health 25, 26
Hebrew Dispersion 77
Hebrew 95
Herod 11, 13, 28
Herodians 105, 114
Hill of Ares 81–82
Hillel 20–21
Hittites 24
Horace 9, 15, 31, 97, 100

Huns 11
Ides of March 51
idolatry 82–83, 106
incense routes 13
inn 21–22
Isaiah 23, 116
Israelites 95
Jerusalem 18
Jesus 9, 11, 17–18, 21, 22–26, 25, 78, 95–96, 102, 103, 104, 109, 110, 113
Jewish Dispersion 97
Jewish rebellion 37–38
Jewry, global 97
Jews, Hellenistic 77, 97
Jews 64, 66–68, 78, 95–102
Jezebel 125
John the Baptist 22, 23, 116–117
Joseph of Arimathea 11–12
Joseph 19–22, 26
Josephus 23, 44, 59, 95, 103
Judas Maccabeus 95
Judea 17, 44
Julius Caesar 11, 13, 14
Juvenal 33, 43, 97, 100, 121
Ladder of Tyre 24
language, Greek 106
law 104, 109
lead-poisoning 25
legalism 106–108
Livy 53
Luke 27, 28, 29, 39, 45, 98
Lystra 42
Macedon 50
Maecenas 9
Marcus Aurelius 90
Marcus Antonius 51
Mary 18, 19–22, 26
Masada 117
Matthew 27
medical practice 26
Mediterranean Sea 11–12
Megiddo Pass 24
Megiddo 21, 24
Mithras 29, 101
monastery, Qumran (illus.) 115
Moses 101
mythology, Greek 79

Nabataeans 13, 28
names 78
Nazareth 22–26
Nero 32, 43, 117, 121
Nicodemus 104, 123–127
Octavian 47, 51
Onesimus 32, 56
oral law 104, 106, 112
paganism 125
pagans 120
Palestine (map) 65
Palestine 17–30
Pallas 70
pantheism 89
Parthenon 82, 91
Parthian shot 13
Parthians 13, 24, 55–56
Parthia 13
Passover 99
Paul 11–12, 33, 44, 48, 56–58, 69, 81–86, 86, 88, 92, 96, 99, 106, 109, 112, 120–121, 123
Pax Romanus 9
Peace, Roman 47
people, common 31–38
persecution 121–123
Peter 109
Petronius 31–32
Pharisees 103–113
Philip 97
Philip the Second 75
phusis 89–90
Pilate, Pontius 25, 66–69
Piso 87
Pliny 114–115, 122
Pompey 51
poor, the 34–35
Porcius Festus 45, 69–73
poverty 33
preaching 101–102
Priscilla 11
procurators 63–64, 66
Quintilius Varus 27–29
Quirinius, Publius Sulpicius 14, 27–28, 29, 42, 64
Qumran 22, 23, 114, 116–117
Qumran (illus. 115)
Rachel 20

rainfall 25
Ramsay, Sir William 54, 39–40, 126
Revelation 13
Rhine River 14
rivers 14–15
roads 57–58
Roman Empire 47–54
Roman Empire (map) 10
Roman frontiers 11
Roman Peace (see: Pax Romanus)
Rome 120
Royal Porch 91
Sabbath 106–107
Sadducees 103, 105, 111–114, 116
Sahara 12
sailing 59, 61
Samaria 17
Samaritans 36
Sanhedrin 111–112, 104–105, 45
Saul 45
scribes 104
Scriptures 98, 100, 115
Seianus 19, 36
Septuagint 77
Sermon on the Mount 34–35
sermons 101–102
sewers, sewer systems 25
shipbuilding 61
ships 58–61
Sicily 49
Silanus, M. Julius 41
Simeon 20–21
Simon 12
slaves, slavery 32
Spain 49–50
spear 36
Spirit of Masada, The 64
Stephen 43, 45
Stoicism 86, 88, 89, 90
Switzerland 14
Sychar well 36
synagogue 96–100
Tacitus 44
Talmud 23
Talmud, Babylon 107
Talmud, Jerusalem 107

Temple 106, 113
Tenth Legion 26
Teutones 11
The West 15
Thessalonica 120
Thothmes III 24
Tiberius 14
trade routes (map) 60
Trajan 90
travel 55–61
trial of Christ 68–69
tribute-money 66–67

Unknown God 81, 90
Vergil 15, 97
water pollution 25
water 25
weather 25–26
Wingless Victory 83, 91
written law 112
Yemen 56
Zadok 111
Zealot 117
Zeno of Citium 86, 88
Zoroastrianism 105

Scripture Index

Exodus
3:6 .113

Numbers
27:1–11 19
36:1–13 19

Joshua
1:4 11

2 Samuel
19:31–38 21

1 Kings
10:1–22 56

2 Kings
18:26 95
25:25 95

Ezra
6:21 105

Nehemiah
5:8 95
13:24 95

1 Maccabees
2:42 105
7:13 105
8:23, 25, 27 95

2 Maccabees
14:6 105

Psalms
137 .98

Isaiah
29:13 104
36:11 95
61:1 .23

Jeremiah
34:9 .95
38:19 95
41:17 21

Ezekiel
36 .104
37 .104

Matthew
2:11 .13
3 113
4:25 .80
5:17 .96
6:6 35
6:19 .35
8:4 96
15:21–28 96
16:1 105
16:1–4 12
16:1, 6, 11, 12 113
20:1–16 35
22:15, 16 105
22:16 114
22:23–33 113
23:13–39 104
24:23–26 64
27:19 68

Mark
2:23–28 96
3:1–5 96
3:6 .105
3:6 .114
4:38 .61
7:6, 7 104
7:8–13 104
7:24–30 96

Reference	Page
12:13	105, 114
12:18–27	113
14:53–15:5	113
15:21	12, 57
15:36	36
15:43	104

Luke

Reference	Page
2:1	16
2:47	25
4:18–19	34
5:7	61
7:4, 5	99
7:36–38	104
10:30–35	36
11:5–8	35
11:37	104
13:31	104
14:1	104
15:8–10	35
17:10	104
18:18–24	34
19:32	41
19:38	41
20:27–38	113
23:6, 7	69
23:50–53	104

John

Reference	Page
1	105, 113
1:11	18
1:47	23
2:14–18	113
3	104
6:13	78
7:35	77
7:47–49	109
7:50	104
9	105
11	96
11:49, 50	114
11:57	113
12:20	77, 78
19:29	36
19:38	104
19:39	104
20:19	96

Acts

Reference	Page
2	98
2:5–11	56
4:1–22	113
5:17–42	113
5:34–39	104
5:37	27, 64
6:1	78
8:27–38	97
9:29	78
11:20	77, 78
11:26	96
11:28	12
13:14, 15	101
14:1	77
15:41	58
16:1	77
16:12	58
16:13	98
16:14	56
16:37, 38	71
16:9–12	56
17	81
17:4, 12	77
17:5	121
17:11	100
17:21	57
17:22–28	100
18:4	77
19	122
19:10, 17	77
20:3	99
20:13, 14	58
20:21	77
21	45
21:28	77
22:25–27, 29	71
22:26	70
23:6–10	112
23:12, 13	108
24:2, 3	70
27:1	58
27:9–12	28
27:17	61
28:14, 15	99
28:15	58

Romans

Reference	Page
1:14	77
2:17–29	96
9:6	96

15:21 12
15:24 120

1 Corinthians
1:22–24 77

2 Corinthians
11:25, 26 58

Galatians
2:14 96
3:29 96

Philippians
4:22 33

1 Timothy
5:23 25

James
4:13 56

1 Peter
4:4 121
4:7, 12 .48

2 Peter
3:15, 16 123

Revelation
2 . . . . 120, 123
2:9 96
3 . . . . 120, 123
9:7–11 .13
13 125